"In a day in which the public ~~reading of Scripture is ne~~glected by far too many, I rejoice to see this work. I pray that it will influence a new generation of leaders to restore this historic practice in corporate worship."

—Tony Merida,
Associate Professor of Preaching,
Southeastern Baptist Theological Seminary

"I strongly encourage pastors who value the Word of God to read this book on how to read Scripture well. Jeff Arthurs uplifts the Word of God, and he will convince you of the importance of reading Scripture publicly and coach you how to read it better. You will also enjoy the concise review of what makes for effective communication."

—Randal Emery Pelton,
Senior Pastor, Calvary Bible Church,
Mount Joy, PA

"I am thrilled with Arthurs's emphasis on a lost aspect of worship. I will never forget the impression that the public reading of Philippians made on me as a teenager. Instead of preaching, our guest speaker simply read Paul's letter to the people at Philippi. When he finished, the whole church sat quietly, obviously moved by the Spirit of God. The effect was powerful and used by God. May a similar high respect for the reading aloud of the Word of God return to our churches and homes once again."

—Walter C. Kaiser Jr.,
President Emeritus,
Gordon-Conwell Theological Seminary

"Good on Jeff Arthurs for reminding us that we actually need to be present with people in the presentation of the Word. Our technologies create distance. Devoting ourselves to the physical reading of Scripture is a prime way of seeing the Word incarnate among people. This practical, well-researched book helps us remember how."

Kenton C. Anderson,
President,
Northwest Baptist Seminary

"Jeffrey Arthurs builds a compelling case for a biblically mandated but embarrassingly neglected ministry—public Scripture reading. The book is not only biblical, reminding the reader of commonly overlooked texts that bear on the subject, it is also up-to-date, informative, well documented, clearly illustrated, unfailingly wise, and eminently helpful. I found excellence on every turn of the page. I can't recommend it too highly."

Greg R. Scharf,
Professor of Pastoral Theology,
Trinity Evangelical Divinity School

"I enthusiastically recommend Jeffrey Arthurs's new book, which seeks to restore a central element of New Testament and early Christian worship—the serious, intentional, public reading of God's inspired Word. I commend this work to pastors, seminarians, and to all those who are privileged to read the Scriptures in public worship."

John Jefferson Davis,
Professor of Systematic Theology & Christian Ethics,
Gordon-Conwell Theological Seminary

"I wholeheartedly recommend this book!"

Craig Brian Larson,
Editor,
PreachingToday.com

"God created the universe with the power of his spoken word and continues to refashion lives where his Word is heard today. Jeffrey Arthurs serves the church well by showing us why and how to read God's powerful words."

J. Kent Edwards,
Professor of Preaching & Leadership,
Talbot School of Theology

"Engaging the audience in the beginning of a sermon can be difficult. A preacher may feel like he is pulling a heavy carriage that refuses to move. If you have similar experiences, *Devote Yourself to the Public Reading of Scripture* is a must read for Scripture readers or worship leaders. Dr. Jeffrey Arthurs provides us a biblical, pastoral, and practical presentation for giving God's Word its rightful place in our worship. Put into practice the insights and wisdom in this book, and you may find the carriage already moving when you get up to the pulpit."

Henry Chan,
Pastor, The Rutgers Community Christian Church,
Somerset, NJ

"We drain away the power of the Word with its unpracticed, and uninspired public reading. We put more thought into the announcements than we do the reading of the Word; we invest hours in music rehearsals but read the Bible without so much as a once-through. But imagine a Scripture reading that was as fresh as rain, as weighty as stone tablets, as surgical as a blade, and as welcoming as a Father's letter to a long-lost child. Imagine that, and then read Dr. Jeffrey Arthurs's book to see how it could happen in your church."

Lee Eclov,
Senior Pastor, Village Church,
Lincolnshire, IL

"Many churches have tampered with the public reading, preaching, and teaching of Scripture (1 Tim. 4:13). The public reading of Scripture is the most neglected of the three, and in some churches it is omitted altogether. With thoughtful theological reflection and sound communication theory, Jeffrey Arthurs demonstrates in a practical way how Scripture reading can become the spiritual starburst of the worship service. Well-researched, this book is packed with creative ideas balanced with pastoral sensitivity. Sample scripts and a DVD also add value to this helpful resource."

—Rock LaGioia,
Associate Professor of Pastoral Studies,
Grace Theological Seminary

"Jeff Arthurs will delightfully take you from the history and power of reading Scripture out loud, to specific skills for doing it well, to varied and creative ways of including it in worship. He has given us a wealth of information and ideas."

Don Sunukjian,
Professor of Preaching,
Talbot School of Theology

Devote Yourself
to the
Public Reading
of Scripture

The Transforming Power of the Well-Spoken Word

Jeffrey D. Arthurs

Kregel
Academic & Professional

Devote Yourself to the Public Reading of Scripture: The Transforming Power of the Well-Spoken Word

© 2012 by Jeffrey D. Arthurs

A digital edition of this book and the contents of the DVD in a downloadable format are available from www.kregel.com.

Published by Kregel Publications, a division of Kregel, Inc., P.O. Box 2607, Grand Rapids, MI 49501.

ISBN 978-0–8254-4219-3

Printed in the United States of America
12 13 14 15 16 / 5 4 3 2 1

CONTENTS

ACKNOWLEDGEMENTS

This book has been in the making for thirty years—ever since my college speech teacher took me aside and suggested that I double major in Bible and speech communication. His counsel set me on a track that led me to write this brief book on the oral interpretation of Scripture.

Over the course of those thirty years, I racked up quite a few debts of gratitude.

My love of oral reading began with my father who read aloud to my brother and me as we curled on the couch beside him. We loved *I Robot* by Isaac Asimov but giggled at "The Wreck of the Hesperus" by Edgar Allen Poe.

The college speech teacher who took me aside was Lonnie Polson, who later served as leader of the evangelistic drama team I traveled with. Other university professors of speech, literature, and rhetoric were Don Ryerson and DeWitt Jones. Now deceased are Joyce Parks, Robert Pratt, and Elizabeth Edwards. In those days giants walked the land.

In seminary I learned that the Bible is not just a book of ancient languages and deep theology but also of beautiful literature. James Sweeney and Jim

Andrews pointed more toward this way of thinking. During my doctoral work, I was encouraged by Don Burks, whose own interest in rhetoric began, like mine, with the performance of literature. In teaching positions after that I collaborated with colleagues Miriam Gibby and Shawna Reed to create programs of music, drama, and Scripture. Hunter Barnes, my friend and colleague, has put the theory of oral interpretation into practice with his powerful reading of the book of Mark. Students like John Voelz and Drew Thompson have influenced me as much as my teachers. And colleagues Scott Gibson and Haddon Robinson have modeled biblical preaching that combines creativity and fidelity. My friend and editor Jim Weaver has encouraged me without fail, and my dear wife, Liz, the most delightful person I know, has modeled excellence both as a student and as a public reader of the Word.

Thanks be to God for giving us Holy Scripture.

INTRODUCTION

IN *Eat This Book*, Eugene Peterson compares Scripture reading to preparing, serving, and eating a meal in community.[1] I like that metaphor, and I allude to it in the chapter titles of this book. The Word of God is bread for our souls, and we are fed when we hear the Word well read. Unfortunately, when it is not read well, listeners do not ingest it. Scripture reading is often the low point of an already lethargic service. Surveys of church members rank the public reading of Scripture as one of the dullest portions of the gathering.[2] To be sure, the "feel" of a meeting is not the only (or best) standard of effectiveness, but neither should we reject it as "unspiritual." Leaders would do well to ask if listeners tune out during Scripture reading. If the answer is yes, they would do well to change something. This book can help.

My vision is to increase the quantity and the quality of Scripture reading in church services. We need to do more of it, and we need to do a better

---

1. Eugene H. Peterson, *Eat This Book: A Conversation in the Art of Spiritual Reading* (Grand Rapids: Eerdmans, 2006), 72.
2. David and Karen Mains, "Down with the Dulls: Bringing Public Scripture Reading to Life," audio CD, n. d.

job of it. Most of the time I have in mind the Sunday morning service, but the principles fit other contexts as well—weddings, funerals, concerts, classes, coffee houses, etc. This book is for anyone who reads Scripture in public or oversees gatherings where it is read.

Because Scripture reading is better caught than taught—better demonstrated than described—a DVD accompanies this book where you can see me demonstrate many of the ideas and techniques described in the book.

In my role as professor at Gordon-Conwell Theological Seminary, I teach preaching and communication, and I provide training to pastors and lay leaders on Scripture reading. For nine years I was also the dean of the chapel. I'm an elder in my church, and I lead a Scripture reading team there. My background includes degrees in Bible and speech with an emphasis in oral interpretation— the art of reading aloud from the page. I love the spoken word, and I have seen how powerful it is when the reader gives heart and mind to the author's creation.

May God use this book to help his people devote themselves to the public reading of his Word.

Thank you for reading.

1
—

Building an Appetite

"There is a millennia-deep and globe-encircling community of others who are also at the table eating this book."[1]

—Eugene Peterson

Eugene Peterson compares Scripture reading to a feast. To enjoy a feast we begin by building an appetite. We're going to "build an appetite" for the public reading of Scripture by developing a taste for this specially prepared, spiritually nutritious meal.

If you're already convinced that the ministry of Scripture reading is crucial to the spiritual health of individuals and churches, this chapter will strengthen your stance. If you're not convinced, read on!

---

1. Eugene H. Peterson, *Eat This Book: A Conversation in the Art of Spiritual Reading* (Grand Rapids: Eerdmans, 2006), 72.

In many churches, public reading of the Bible is little more than homiletical throat-clearing before the sermon. Fred Craddock states, "For all the noises ministers make about the centrality of the Bible in the church, the public reading of Scripture in many places does not support that conviction."[2]

He's right. Many churches that pride themselves on being "Bible churches" feature very little of God's Holy Word. Not only do we relegate Scripture reading to the fringe of "what really matters" in our services, but even when we do read, we often read poorly.

The place we give to public reading reminds us that the way we worship forms what we believe (*lex ordandi lex credendi*).

When the Bible is read well, it can minister as deeply as a Spirit-empowered sermon. Hearing the Word read without commentary reminds us that God inspired the Word and now illumines those who hear it. As theologian John Davis states, "Taking seriously the public reading of Scripture is a way of acknowledging the freedom of God to speak to us directly apart from the human preacher."[3]

The five arguments in this chapter whet our appetites for an increase in the quantity and quality of our public reading.

---

2. Fred B. Craddock, *Preaching* (Nashville: Abingdon, 1985), 210.

3. John Jefferson Davis, *Worship and the Reality of God: An Evangelical Theology of Real Presence* (Downers Grove, IL: InterVarsity, 2010), 103.

ARGUMENT #1—We are commanded to read the Bible publicly: "Devote yourself to the public reading" (1 Tim. 4:13). The word "devote" (Gk. *prosecho*) means to "hold the mind toward" or "pay attention to, give heed to, or apply oneself."

Paul's command to Timothy needs to be understood in light of first-century culture when few people knew how to read and very few manuscripts existed. That was a day of chirography (hand writing), not typography (mechanically produced texts). If a pastor wanted to build up his people in the most holy faith, it was mandatory that he read the Bible aloud.

In contrast, nearly everyone in today's Western Church can read and most have multiple copies of the Bible. However, literacy and abundance of Bibles does not mean that we're actually reading them. Biblical literacy may be lower today than it was in the first century. Summarizing general themes on spirituality in America for the year 2009, the Barna organization concluded: "Biblical literacy is neither a current reality nor a goal in the U.S."[4] This helps account for the fact that Americans, including those who go to church regularly, do not have a Christian worldview. According to Barna, only nineteen percent of born-again people

---

4. http://www.barna.org/barna-update/article/12-faithspirituality/325-barna-studies-the-research-offers-a-year-in-review-perspective, accessed Aug. 4, 2010.

have a Christian worldview.[5] We are ignorant of God's promises and requirements.

Even when church goers *are* aware of those promises and requirements, they need regular reminders. C. S. Lewis captures this dynamic in *The Silver Chair*. Aslan commands Jill to "seek this lost Prince until either you have found him and brought him to his father's house, or else died in the attempt."[6]

> "How, please?" said Jill.
> "I will tell you, Child," said the Lion. "These are the Signs by which I will guide you in your quest."

The four Signs that Aslan gives to Jill are a mixture of clear specifics and vague generalities. But they are sufficient. Aslan sends her on the quest with this exhortation:

> Remember, remember, the Signs. Say them to yourself when you wake in the morning and when you lie down at night, and when you wake in the middle of the night. And whatever strange things may happen to you, let nothing turn your mind from following the Signs. . . . I give you a warning. Here on the mountain

5. Ibid.
6. C. S. Lewis, *The Silver Chair* (New York: Macmillan, 1953), 19–21.

I have spoken to you clearly: I will not often do so down in Narnia. Here on the mountain, the air is clear and your mind is clear; as you drop down into Narnia, the air will thicken. Take great care that it does not confuse your mind. . . . Remember the Signs and believe the Signs. Nothing else matters.

If you have read the marvelous *Chronicles*, you know that Jill and her friend Eustace vault from one adventure to another. At first Jill is faithful in reviewing the Signs daily, but gradually she lets them slide. She mixes up the wording, forgets sections, and does not use them when she has to make decisions. It results in near disaster, but thankfully, she remembers and obeys enough to help her fulfill the quest.

The air here is thick and our minds are often befogged. We need to be reminded, so God commands us to read Scripture publicly. This is a way of helping God's people follow the Signs.

ARGUMENT #2—God transforms us through the Word. The Word of God is a fire that burns away dross (Jer. 23:29), a hammer that breaks stony hearts (Jer. 23:9), rain that waters crops (Isa. 55:10–11), milk that nourishes babies (1 Pet. 2:2), food that fills the hungry (Heb. 5:12–13), a sword that pierces the heart and battles the devil (Heb. 4:12; Eph. 6:17), gold that enriches us (Ps 19:10), a mirror that shows us our true selves (James 1:23–25), and a lamp that illumines our path (Ps. 119:105; Prov. 6:23; 2 Pet. 1:19).

Our belief in the power of the Word will influence our practice. Would a visitor to your worship services conclude that you believe in announcements more than the Word? Or in skillful music more than skillful reading? Although announcements can be useful and skillful music is delightful, let us not neglect the Word! The quantity and quality of our reading demonstrates whether or not we expect God to transform us through the Word which is "living and active" (Heb. 4:12). God's Word has power to create, rule, and redeem.[7]

CONCERNING CREATION
By the word of the Lord the heavens were made (Ps. 33:6).

CONCERNING RULING
Forever, O Lord, your word is firmly fixed in the heavens. Your faithfulness endures to all generations; you have established the earth, and it stands fast. By your appointment they stand this day (Ps. 119:89–91).

He sends out his command to the earth; his

---

7. Dallas Willard, *Hearing God: Developing a Conversational Relationship With God* (Downers Grove, IL: InterVarsity, 1993), 118.

word runs swiftly. He gives snow like wool; he scatters hoarfrost like ashes (Ps. 147:15–16).

CONCERNING REDEMPTION

They cried to the Lord in their trouble, and he saved them from their distress; he sent out his word and healed them, and delivered them from destruction (Ps. 107:19–20).

We are born again, not of perishable but of imperishable seed, through the living and enduring word of God (1 Pet. 1:23).

He gave us birth by the word of truth" (James 1:18) which "has the power to save your souls" (James 1:23) by the "washing of water by the word" (Eph. 5:26).

No wonder Mahatma Gandhi said, "You Christians look after a document containing enough dynamite to blow all civilization to pieces, turn the world upside down and bring peace to a battle-torn planet. But you treat it as though it is nothing more than a piece of good literature."[8]

ARGUMENT #3—When we read the Bible publicly, we do what the people of God have al-

---

8. In Max McLean and Warren Bird, *Unleashing the Word: Rediscovering the Public Reading of Scripture* (Grand Rapids: Zondervan, 2009), 67.

ways done. As Eugene Peterson says, "There is a millennia-deep and globe-encircling community of others who are also at the table eating this book."[9] In earliest times God communicated by voice and visions. Then a critical shift came when Israel left Egypt. The Word of God was written down. Ephemeral sound was calcified in script, and oral repetition of that script became the center of worship as Israel regularly renewed its covenant with God.[10]

- Public reading and renewing of the covenant began when Moses received the law of God:

  Moses came and told the people all the words of the Lord and all the rules. And all

---

9. Peterson, *Eat This Book*, 72.
10. Much of the material in this section comes from Timothy J. Ralston, "Scripture in Worship: An Indispensable Symbol of Covenant Renewal," in *Authentic Worship: Hearing Scripture's Voice, Applying Its Truths*, Herbert W. Bateman, IV, ed. (Grand Rapids: Kregel, 2002), 195–222; Bryan Chapell, "The Incarnate Voice: An Exhortation for Excellence in the Oral Reading of Scripture," *Presbyterion* vol. 15, no. 1 (Spring, 1989): 42–57; and Bryan Chapell, "A Brief History of Scripture Reading," in *Resources for Music and the Arts*, vol. 4, *The Topical Encyclopedia of Christian Worship* (Nashville: Abbott-Martyn, 1993): 696–98. The articles by Chapell are edited and reproduced in Bryan Chapell, *Christ-Centered Worship: Letting the Gospel Shape Our Practice* 2nd edition (Grand Rapids: Baker, 2009), 220–33. See also, *Twenty Centuries of Christian Worship*, Robert E. Webber, ed., Vol. 2 in *The Complete Library of Christian Worship* (Nashville: Star Song, 1994).

the people answered with one voice and said, "The words that the Lord has spoken we will do." And Moses wrote down all the words of the Lord. . . . Then he took the Book of the Covenant and read it in the hearing of all the people (Ex. 24:3–4, 7).

- Public reading continued at the end of Moses' life as he instructed the nation:

At the end of every seven years . . . at the Feast of Booths, when all Israel comes to appear before the Lord your God . . . you shall read this law before all Israel in their hearing. Assemble the people, men, women and little ones, and the sojourner within your towns, that they may hear and learn to fear the Lord your God, and be careful to do all the words of this law, and that their children, who have not known it, may hear and learn to fear the Lord your God (Deut. 31:10–13).

Notice that this command was given to Israel while they were still encamped on the plains of Moab. The command envisions Israel as already settled in the Promised Land, having been there for multiple cycles of seven years. Thus, Moses' command was addressed to future generations as much as it was to those gathered before him.

- Joshua carried on the program of public reading as Israel entered the Promised Land:

  > In the presence of the people of Israel, [Joshua] wrote on the stones a copy of the law of Moses . . . . And all Israel, sojourner as well as native born, with their elders and officers and their judges, stood on opposite sides of the ark of the covenant of the Lord, half of them on Mount Gerazim and half of them stood in front of Mount Ebal. . . . He read all the words of the law. . . . There was not a word of all that Moses commanded that Joshua did not read before all the assembly" (Josh. 8:30–35).

- As the nation was established in the Promised Land, Scripture reading was prominent at the annual festivals of Passover, Firstfruits, and Booths when all Israelite males were required to "present themselves before the Lord" (Ex. 23:14–17), an expression that was shorthand for covenant renewal. Thus Robert Webber concludes that "Jewish worship has always had Scripture at the center of its worship."[11]

- Over time, the Word was forgotten and the people slipped into idolatry. Israel no longer re-

---

11. Robert E. Webber, *Worship Is a Verb* (Dallas: Word, 1985), 74–75.

22

viewed and remembered the Signs. While they still offered sacrifices, they did not celebrate Passover (2 Kings 23:22–23, 2 Chron. 35:18) or the other festivals, and thus did not hear about their covenant relationship and stipulations. The prophets corroborate this picture (Isa. 5:13; Jer. 4:22; Hos. 4:1, 6, 14; Mal. 2:1–9). Then, under good king Josiah, the Word was redis- covered. Shaphan read the Law in the presence of the king, and the king called all the people together "from the least to the greatest" and he "read in their hearing all the words of the Book of the Covenant" (2 Kings 23:2).

- During the Exile, Israelites living outside Pales- tine lifted the Law to new heights. Away from the Temple and altar, they studied how the Law applied to them in pagan surroundings. The synagogue was born and the Jews met weekly, not just during annual festivals, to hear the Word read.

- After the Exile, revival took place under Ezra as the people heard the Word of God:

> Ezra opened the book in the sight of all the people. . . . And Ezra blessed the Lord, the great God, all the people answered, 'Amen, Amen,' lifting their hands. And they bowed their heads and worshiped the Lord with their faces to the ground. . . . They read

from the book, from the Law of God, clearly, and they gave the sense, so that the people understood the reading (Neh. 8:5–8).

- About the time of Christ, synagogue worship included readings from multiple passages— the Law, the Prophets, and the Writings. Jesus read part of one of those passages as he inaugurated his ministry (Luke 4: 16–18). Similarly, Paul preached in Antioch of Pisidia after the readings of the Law and Prophets (Acts 13:15–16; cf. Acts 15:21). In Palestine, the Torah was read in cycles of roughly three and a half years.[12] While reading of Scripture was crucial to synagogue worship, as it still is today, the sermon was optional.[13] Sorry, fellow preachers!

- The New Testament Church continued the synagogue practice of public reading of the Hebrew Bible and added the writings of the apostles as well. Thus, Paul commanded Timothy, "Devote yourself to the public reading" (1 Tim. 4:13). He says, in effect, to continue the "millennia-deep" tradition. Paul's first

---

12. Michael Graves, "The Public Reading of Scripture in Early Judaism," *Journal of the Evangelical Theological Society,* vol. 50, no. 3 (Sept. 2007): 473.
13. Arthur T. Piersen, *How to Read the Word of God Effectively* (Chicago: Moody, 1925), 3-4; J. Edward Lantz, *Reading the Bible Aloud* (New York: Macmillan, 1959), 3.

letter to Timothy, a manual for church leaders, implies that devoting ourselves to public reading helps teach and maintain the faith. Paul's use of the definite article, referring to "*the* faith," implies that we have a fixed body of doctrine that all believers should understand and to which all should give assent (1 Tim. 3:9; 4:1, 6; 6:21).

- The Church Fathers sat at the table also. Justin Martyr, in Rome in the mid-second century, said that in their services folk gathered to hear the Scriptures read "as long as time permits."[14] Bryan Chapell states that "by the end of the fourth-century the dominant liturgical pattern included three readings: one from the Old Testament and two from the New—an epistle and a gospel. The last reading was always the gospel, and the people stood during this reading."[15] Some lectionaries of Mesopotamia had four lessons for public reading, others had six, and feast days probably stipulated even more readings.[16] If you attended one of those Mesopotamian churches

---

14. Justin Martyr, *1 Apology* 67, in Ralston, "Scripture in Worship," 208.
15. Chapell, "A Brief History of Scripture Reading," 697.
16. Hughes Oliphant Old, *The Reading and Preaching of the Scriptures in the Worship of the Christian Church*, vol. 2 (Grand Rapids: Eerdmans, 1998), 277.

you would hear an average of fifty to eighty verses each Sunday.[17]

- Early in the fourth century, the office of "reader" was one of the ministerial roles. Albert Newman writes in *A Manual of Church History*, "The duty of *readers* was to read the Scriptures from the reading desk. Very few Christians had copies of the Scriptures, and the great mass of the people were dependent upon hearing them read at church."[18] The scarcity of written Scripture elevated the value of the spoken Word.

- During the Reformation, a movement marked by a return to the Word, the Anabaptist movement stands out. John Christian comments: "Among the skilled artisans, journeyman and better situated peasants of the early sixteenth century, there were not a few who could read sufficiently to make out the text of the German Bible, whilst those who could not read would form a circle around those who could, and the latter, from the [coin] of intellectual advantage, would not merely read, but would often expound the text after their own fashion

---

17. Old, *Reading and Preaching of the Scriptures*, 282.
18. Albert Henry Newman, *A Manual of Church History*, rev. ed. (Valley Forge, PA: Judson, 1933), 1:294.

to the hearers."[19] These informal Bible readings became a hallmark of the Baptists.

- Puritan services in the American colonies about the time of Jonathan Edwards (mid-1700s) read an Old Testament lesson, a New Testament lesson, each at least a chapter in length, and sang a metrical psalm.[20] As the *Directory for the Public Worship of God* specified, "How large a portion shall be read at once, is left to the wisdome of the Minister: but it is convenient, that ordinarily a Chapter of each Testament bee read at every meeting [three times a week]; and sometimes more, where the Chapters be short, or the coherence of matter requireth it."[21]

Based on the prominence that public reading of Scripture has had through the millennia, Timothy Ralston concludes that it is crucial in helping people remember the Signs, or in his words: "Public reading within the worship exposes His demands, their inadequacy, and His grace. It calls for covenant renewal and lies at the heart of spiritual revival. Therefore, how can we offer acceptable

---

19. John T. Christian, *A History of the Baptists* (Texarkana, TX: Bogard, 1922), 102–103.
20. Douglas A. Sweeney, *Jonathan Edwards and the Ministry of the Word; A Model of Faith and Thought* (Downers Grove, IL: InterVarsity, 2009), 58.
21. In Sweeney, *Jonathan Edwards*, 58–59.

worship, if His Word does not have a prominent place in our liturgy?"[22]

ARGUMENT #4—The Bible was meant to be read aloud. Before it was inscribed on vellum and papyrus, the stories, proverbs, and poetry of the Bible circulated orally, and after the oral literature was written down, it continued to be transmitted orally. Literature in the ancient world was spoken, not read silently, even when someone was reading privately. That is the reason Philip knew the Ethiopian eunuch was reading Isaiah before joining him in his chariot (Acts 8:27). And the celebrated passage from Augustine's *Confessions*,[23] where he happened upon Ambrose who was

---

22. Ralston, "Scripture in Worship," 209.
23. Book 6, Chapter 3. The Harvard Classics edition is available at http://www.bartleby.com/7/1/6.html. The passage I have in mind states: "When [Ambrose] was reading, his eye glided over the pages, and his heart searched out the sense, but his voice and tongue were at rest. Ofttimes when we had come . . . we saw him thus reading to himself, and never otherwise; and having long sat silent (for who durst intrude on one so intent?) we were fain to depart, conjecturing that in the small interval which he obtained, free from the din of others' business . . . he was loth to be taken off; and perchance he dreaded lest . . . some attentive or perplexed hearer should desire him to expound [the book], or to discuss some of the harder questions; so that his time being thus spent, he could not turn over so many volumes as he desired; although the preserving of his voice (which a very little speaking would weaken) might be the truer reason for his reading to himself. But with what intent soever he did it, certainly in such a man it was good."

reading privately, also reflects the fact that reading aloud was the norm. In fact, even among scholars, reading silently became common only in the tenth century.[24] Thus the Bible, indeed all ancient literature, is an "arrested performance," like a musical score.[25]

The Bible alludes to its aural quality when it says, "I warn everyone who *hears* the words of the prophecy of this book" (Rev. 22:18) and "Long ago God spoke to our fathers in many and various ways by the prophets, but in these last days he has spoken to us by his Son . . . . Therefore we must pay greater attention to *what we have heard*" (Heb.1:1–2, 2:1). Even epistles, the genre that may seem to be most coupled to writing, were prepared orally in community, then dictated orally to a scribe, and then delivered orally to the

---

24. Alberto Manguel, *The History of Reading* (New York: Viking, 1996). Page Available at http://www.stanford.edu/class/history34q/readings/Manguel/Silent_Readers.html. Walter Ong places the date even later—the eighteenth century. He states, "Manuscript culture in the West was always marginally oral, and, even after print, textually only gradually achieved the place it has today in cultures where most reading is silent. We have not yet come to full terms with the fact that from antiquity well through the eighteenth century many literary texts, even when composed in writing, were commonly for public recitation; originally by the author himself." *Orality and Literacy: The Technologizing of the Word* (New York: Metheun, 1982), 154.

25. Beverly Whitaker Long and Mary Frances HopKins, *Performing Literature: An Introduction to Oral Interpretation* (Englewood Cliffs, NJ: Prentice-Hall, 1982), 2.

intended audience through public reading.[26] For example, the letter to believers living in Colossae reads: "When this letter has been read among you, have it also read in the church of the Laodiceans" (Col. 4:16). Even a letter like Philemon, the most personal of all New Testament epistles, was read aloud to the church that met in his home (vv. 1–2).

The Bible originated as oral communication, was then inscripturated (written down), and was then transmitted from voice to ear. This is still the case today in much of the Church. Of the three thousand or so languages, only about eighty have a written literature.[27] One researcher, Dave McClellan, estimates that for ninety percent of God's people, personal texts of the Bible were virtually unknown for commoners.[28] He states:

> Most of the people of God, for most of sacred history, have had to get along in the faith without the benefit of a personal Bible or any sustained and systematic obligation to read it for themselves. Somehow common folk were converted, prayed, parented, served, evangelized, learned Biblical content, and activated their

---

26. See Jeffrey D. Arthurs, *Preaching With Variety: How to Recreate the Dynamics of Biblical Genres* (Grand Rapids: Kregel, 2007), 162–65.

27. Dave T. McClellan, *Recovering a Classically Oral Homiletic* (unpub. diss., Duquesne Univ., 2009), 37.

28. McClellan, *Recovering a Classically Oral Homiletic*, 69.

faith in the world using only the oral/aural reception of the word of God that they heard articulated from the synagogue or parish lectern.[29]

This is not an argument to return to the "good old days," but it is an argument that throughout history the Bible was read aloud in public, and even today we should include large doses of such reading to augment private reading. Quoting Harris, McClellan continues: "The church's leaders recognized that if Christian writings were to have much effect on the masses, they would have to be transmitted orally."[30]

ARGUMENT #5—Hearing the Word is different from reading it silently. In *The Presence of the Word*, theologian and communication scholar Walter Ong demonstrates that in the ancient world, hearing a text was thought of as an encounter with the author in present time and space. In contrast, typography connoted an absent, distant, and abstract author.[31] This leads Eugene Peterson to caution, "Caveat lector!" Let the

---

29. McClellan, *Recovering a Classically Oral Homiletic*, 71.

30. William Harris, *Ancient Literacy* (Cambridge: Harvard University Press, 1989), 305, in McClellan, *Recovering a Classically Oral Homiletic*, 71.

31. Walter J. Ong, *The Presence of the Word: Some Prolegomena for Cultural and Religious History* (Minneapolis: Univ. of Minnesota Press, 1967), 287–324.

reader beware![32] God may show up, and we may encounter him.

Hearing and seeing a reader embody the text is a different experience than silently pondering a script in the privacy of the study. The chart below summarizes some of the differences.

Communication scholars estimate that sixty-five percent of all "social meaning" and ninety-three percent of "emotional meaning" is communicated through the non-verbal channel.[33] That is, what you look like and sound like as you speak are the primary channels for communicating the nature of your relationship with the receiver (social meaning) and how you feel during the communication event (emotional meaning). Simply put, hearing a text read is a much more holistic experience than reading it silently.

Have you heard the Word read well? Vistas of new understanding open. I remember when I heard the entire book of Hebrews recited from memory. I had never understood that Hebrews is about Jesus! He is superior to angels, superior to the Aaronic priesthood, and superior to the Mosaic

---

32. Peterson, *Eat This Book*, 81–89.
33. Randall P. Harrison, "Nonverbal Communication: Exploration into Time, Space, Action, and Object," *Dimensions in Communication*, eds. James H. Campbell and Hal W. Hepler (Belmont, CA: Wadsworth, 1965), 161; and Albert Mehrabian, *Silent Messages* (Belmont, CA: Wadsworth, 1971), 77. These statistics arise from the study of interpersonal communication, but they are also instructive for public communication like oral interpretation of Scripture.

law. So don't let your confidence slip! Similarly, I remember when I heard the book of Mark read from beginning to end. I never understood how kind Jesus was. Words written are caged, but when performed well, they soar. Let us devote ourselves to the public reading of the Word, increasing both the quantity and the quality of this vital ministry.

A Comparison of Written and Oral Communication	
The Bible as Written Text	The Bible as Spoken Message
Perceived with the eyes.	Perceived with multiple senses—primarily hearing but also sight as we look at the reader and the environment. May use other senses as well.
Interpretation is private, individualistic.	Interpretation is shared, communal.
The rate of communication is under the control of the reader, enabling practices like repetition and skimming.	The rate of communication is under the control of the speaker. The flow of information proceeds like a river which cannot be slowed or accelerated unless the speaker allows it.
Facilitates analysis.	Fosters encounter.
Implies the absence of the author.	Impossible without the presence of the speaker.
Permanent.	Ephemeral. It lasts until the echo fades.
Past.	Present.

2
—

Setting the Table

Bible reading offers the widest scope for the
enrichment of public worship and it is a great pity
that the Scriptures are often so badly read. When
the Book is well read and made to live for the
people, it can do for them what sermons often
fail to do: it can be the very voice of God to their
souls.

—W. E. Sangster, *The Approach to Preaching*[1]

The Holy Scriptures require a humble reader who
shows reverence and fear toward the Word of God
and constantly says, "Teach me, teach me, teach
me."

—Martin Luther, *Table Talk*[2]

---

1. In Al Fasol, *A Guide to Self-Improvement in Delivery* (Grand
   Rapids: Baker, 1983), 81.
2. In Clayton J. Schmidt, *Public Reading of Scripture: A Hand-
   book* (Nashville: Abingdon, 2002), 100.

BEFORE YOU SIT at the table with the "millennia-deep and globe-encircling community," someone needs to set the table. That person is you. This chapter and the next discuss how to prepare to read in public, and the first thing I want to emphasize is that you *should* prepare. Far too often Scripture reading is done without so much as glancing at the passage beforehand. The reader stumbles, fumbles, mumbles, and jumbles the Word of God. This is hardly *devoting* ourselves to the public reading.

Why is lack of preparation so common? Here is a list of reasons that come to mind. Add your own items:

- We think preparation is unnecessary. We talk every day, throughout the day, without practice, so we think, "What's the big deal about reading a passage from the Bible? I know how to talk, don't I? I know how to read, don't I?" The big deal is that reading from a script in public is different from interpersonal, impromptu banter. The first demands that we bend our minds to the ideas and feelings someone else has written; the second demands no bending—we simply think what we are thinking and feel what we are feeling and open the sluice gate of the mouth. The first is mediated, and the second is unmediated. The first is done infrequently; the second is done daily, hourly, or even minute by minute.

- We think that Scripture reading doesn't matter.

The sermon counts! The singing counts! Even the announcements count, but in some churches Bible reading seems superfluous. The unfortunate people in those churches have not heard the Bible read well.

- We procrastinate. We tend to avoid what we fear, and most people fear speaking in public. As the time approaches, therefore, we occupy ourselves with a hundred distracting tasks, thus squandering time for preparation. "Out of sight, out of mind" helps us remain calm. Just ask the ostrich.

- We don't know how to prepare. Fair enough. Read on.

How to Prepare for Public Reading

According to the book of Nehemiah, the Levites "read from the book, from the Law of God, clearly." The word translated "read" is *qara'* meaning to "call, proclaim; to encounter a person." (Neh.8:8). It implies a passionate delivery of truth marked by full conviction, deep feeling, and zealous intensity as in "Jonah began to go into the city. . . . And he *called out*, 'Yet forty days and Nineveh shall be overthrown!'" (Jonah 3:4). Here are some ideas and steps that will help you prepare to read in the spirit of *qara.'*

1. Understand what a Scripture reader does.
Scripture readers stand between two worlds.

The metaphor of two worlds was developed by John Stott to describe preaching,[3] but it applies to public reading as well. The two worlds are the ancient text and the modern audience, and the reader is the bridge. We are the conduit for the ancient author (not to mention the timeless Author) to transport his message to the modern listener.

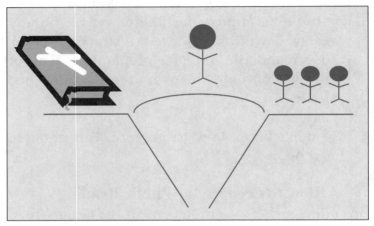

Figure 2.1: Two Worlds

This form of communication is called "oral interpretation," an apt designation because Scripture readers do not create their own message as when an orator develops an original speech. They simply *interpret* what is already given. How we speak the written words—using the pause, emphasis, word color, eye contact, gestures, and so forth—is the

---

3. John Stott, *Between Two Worlds: The Art of Preaching in the Twentieth Century* (Grand Rapids: Eerdmans, 1982).

way we bridge the gap. Public readers of Scripture are organists who play a Bach fugue. They are interpreters, not composers, of the music.

Here is a model similar to Stott's that visualizes what we are trying to do.[4] The text contains ideas and emotions that are impressed on the oral interpreter, who then embodies them for the audience, thus provoking a response.

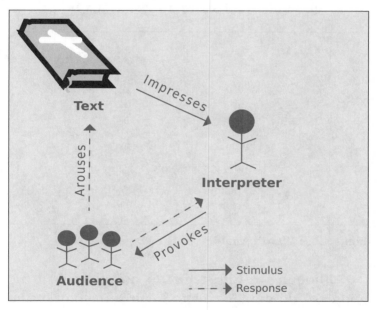

Figure 2.2: A Diagram of Oral Interpretation

Greek philosopoher Plato suggested a model

---

4. Adapted from Todd V. Lewis, *Communicating Literature: An Introduction to Oral Interpretation* (Dubuque, IA: Kendall/ Hunt, 1991), 21.

for this task in his dialogue entitled *Ion*.[5] In Plato's polytheistic and mythological worldview the gods inspire poets who inspire the oral interpreters (or "rhapsodes" as they were known in the ancient Mediterranean world), who in turn inspire the listeners. The power of inspiration is like the power of a magnet transmitting its force through iron rings. From the gods to the poet to the rhapsode to the audience—all share a mysterious bond.

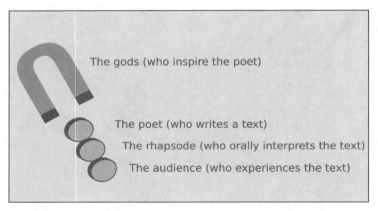

The gods (who inspire the poet)

The poet (who writes a text)

The rhapsode (who orally interprets the text)

The audience (who experiences the text)

Figure 2.3: Plato's Analogy of the Magnet

Although we Christians do not believe in the gods, we do applaud Plato for his analogy of the mysterious, powerful, magnetizing experience of effective oral interpretation.

I approach Scripture reading, as do the creators of the figures above, as a rhetorical act. That is, I believe that public reading should *do* some-

---

5. http://classics.mit.edu/Plato/ion.html.

thing. It should encourage, enable, enlighten, or entreat; it should convict, condemn, console, or convince; it should absolve, abolish, overturn, or undergird. Words are not simply abstract signifiers of concepts. They are a mighty force for good and evil. Life and death are in the power of the tongue (Prov. 18:21). Not only is history recorded in words, it is also made with words, and the oral reader of Scripture is trying to make history, a little bit of history in a small corner of the world. When we serve as conduits, God takes the potential energy of the Word and transforms it into kinetic energy.

If this depiction of what a Scripture reader does sounds too lofty, don't worry; I come down to earth in what follows.

2. Understand what a Scripture reader does *not* do.

We avoid two extremes: a flat, colorless, "aw-shucks" approach that implies, "I'm sorry to take your time, folks; but I have to do this, and it will be over soon"; and an artsy, affected, overblown, theatrical approach that sounds like this: "In the beginning [pause] GAWD created [dramatic gesture] the heavens [eyes rise in a paroxysm of transport] and the 'uhth [fake British accent as the voice sinks to a dramatic whisper]." Which extreme do you tend toward? I tend toward being overly dramatic, and I have found that this is deadly for bridge building. Most people tend toward aw-shucks. We should do neither. Both underselling or overselling lead to bankrupt ministry.

Charlotte Lee, one of the twentieth century's leading figures in the field of oral interpretation, cautions us to avoid overselling:

> The truest and finest art is disarming in its seeming simplicity and its ultimate totality. It makes its observers aware of the result, not the means, used to achieve that result. Technical display is not art. Art is the systematic application of knowledge and skill in effecting a desired result, which in the interpretation of biblical literature, is the effective communication of the Word of God.[6]

We want listeners to pay attention to the Word, not the reader, and overselling calls attention to self. Underselling does too. Aw-shucks readers need to remember the old communication adage: *You cannot not communicate.* Self-conscious fidgeting, hang-dog mumbling, and listless projection send their own messages, and those messages often contradict what should be communicated. Some readers, eager to avoid overselling believe that their flat style is "neutral" or "objective," but Max McLean, who has recorded several audio Bibles, states, "Such so called objectivity is, in real-

---

6. Charlotte I. Lee, *Oral Reading of the Scriptures* (Boston: Houghton Mifflin, 1974), 8.

ity, a carefully considered, established, and maintained point of view that says 'Hands off! Let's not get too involved with this thing.'"[7]

Overblown theatrics and aw-shucks shilly-shallying call attention to the reader rather than to the message of the text.

3. Prepare yourself spiritually.

When God wants to communicate something, he usually embodies that message in a human. He uses incarnation. Thus, as conduits for his Word, we cannot be extracted from the communication process (see the three figures above). This means that we want to be clean vessels for the Master's use. He tells us that "out of the abundance of the heart the mouth speaks" (Matt. 12:34). This is especially true in interpersonal communication, when we generate our own words, but it is also true even when we read someone else's words, as is the case with oral interpretation. Even though the abundance of the heart does not influence *what* words you say, it does influence *how* you say the words already written. The heart that is humble or proud, zealous or cold, selfless or self-centered, rejoicing or grieving, will show its bias.

Here is a short spiritual exercise based on the acronym A.P.C.A.T., which I've adapted from John

---

7. Max McLean and Warren Bird, *Unleashing the Word: Rediscovering the Public Reading of Scripture.* (Grand Rapids: Zondervan, 2009), 66.

Piper.[8] Praying this way before you read Scripture may be helpful.

Admit to the Lord that without him, you can do nothing. Only He can change hearts and bring spiritual growth.

Plead with him to do that work both for yourself and your listeners as you read his Word. Ask him for help.

Claim one of his specific promises that the Word is powerful. Perhaps use one of the metaphors listed in Chapter One—The Word is a fire (Jer. 23:29), a hammer (Jer. 23:9), rain (Isa. 55:10–11), milk (1 Pet. 2:2), food (Heb. 5:12–13), a sword (Heb. 4:12; Eph. 6:17), gold (Ps. 19:10), a mirror (James 1:23–25), and a lamp (Ps. 119:105; Prov. 6:23; 2 Pet. 1:19).

Act in the confidence that God will do as he has promised. Dependence on God's sovereignty does not imply passivity on your part. God has chosen to incarnate his message through humans like Moses, Ezra, Justin Martyr, and you, so exert yourself! Practice your passage, mark your script, check your microphone, and so forth. Follow all the procedures this book details.

---

8. John Piper, *The Supremacy of God in Preaching*, rev. ed. (Grand Rapids: Baker, 2004), 47–49.

Thank him. When your reading is done and he has enabled you to be a good bridge builder, always remember to thank him.

4. Prepare yourself mentally.

You cannot share what you do not possess, and you cannot communicate what you do not know. Effective bridge builders understand what they are reading.

Here's a checklist to help you master the ideas of your text. In most cases, you can do this in thirty to forty minutes.

❏ Read the context of your passage. Understand the flow of the story or the argument so that you see how your portion fits into the whole.

❏ Understand the meanings of all words. Look up unfamiliar ones in study tools, perhaps one of these:

The Zondervan Pictorial Bible Dictionary, Merrill C. Tenny, ed. (Grand Rapids: Zondervan, 1963).

Expository Dictionary of Bible Words, Stephen D. Renn, ed. (Peabody, MA: Henrickson, 2005).

❏ Understand how to pronounce all words. Bible places and names can be tough, but if you devote yourself to this task, you will avoid aw-shucks stumbling that calls attention to itself. To listen to pronunciations, try a website that includes audio such as biblespeech.com or net-ministries.org.

❑ Note words and phrases that reveal structure, such as "the next day," "while they were still speaking," or "but." These help you follow the author's train of thought. Remember that verbs and nouns propel the meaning of sentences. Follow the verbs to get a mental image of the action.

❑ Understand key words and phrases that carry a heavy freight of meaning, such as "sign" in the book of John, "the kingdom of God" throughout the Gospels, and "gospel" in the book of Acts.[9]

❑ Paraphrase. In your practice sessions, state the passage in your own words. This is an excellent way to help you grasp the cognitive content. It helps you "own" it.

---

9. Numerous free online study aids are available. Here are three you might find helpful: Blue Letter Bible at www.blueletter-bible.org; this site contains a wealth of information, including multiple Bible dictionaries and encyclopedias. Into Thy Word at http://70030.netministry.com is another organization that promotes Bible study. See also www.biblegateway.com for more than a dozen English translations.

Mastering the ideational content of your reading is crucial, but remember that texts convey more than ideas. Emotion is present also. We want to orally interpret all that is in the text, not reduce it to a desiccated summary of ideas. Few Bible study books devote much space to understanding affective content, fearing to import subjectivity into the "science" of interpretation. Not doing so can inadvertently rob the Scripture of much of its power and beauty. God did not communicate in bullet points. He used stories, poetry, speeches, letters, visions, and prophecies, and those forms of communication are loaded with emotion.

5. Prepare yourself emotionally.

Have you ever wondered why your heart beats hard when watching a movie as the plot marches toward the climax? Have you ever wondered why a tear comes to your eye when the couple lives happily ever after? Part of the answer is that we identify with the characters. Although the story is fiction and the medium is a two-dimensional projection on a screen, our emotions are engaged. We put ourselves into the story, empathizing with the characters. That is one way art works.

The Bible works that way too. It is literature, and its authors intend for us to identify, imagine, and empathize with the emotions conveyed in the text. For example, the author clearly intends to amaze us with the dramatic miracle of raising Lazarus (John 11). The author clearly intends to astound and relieve us when God parts the Red Sea (Ex. 14). The poet clearly emotes tranquil joy when he describes God as his shepherd (Ps. 23). To accurately and skillfully stand between two worlds we must empathize. Let me say again that I am not advocating a theatrical, overblown approach to Scripture reading but one that conveys the author's intentions. Bishop Whately of England struck the right note: "He should deliver [the Word of God] as if he were reporting another's sentiments, which were both fully understood, and felt in all their force by the reporter."[10] S. S. Curry, a speech teacher from the early twentieth-century, points out the necessity of emotional engagement in the high calling of public reading:

> The reading of the Scriptures must never be perfunctory or merely formal. It should not be a mere authoritative presentation of facts or proclamation of words. . . . The reader must live his ideas at the time of utterance. . . . He can manifest to others the impressions made on his own being. . . . [For] when one soul is made to feel that another soul is hearing a message from the King of kings, he too bows his head and hears the voice of the Infinite speaking in his own breast.[11]

---

10. Richard Whately, *Elements of Rhetoric*, quoted in Bryan Chapell, *Christ-Centered Worship: Letting the Gospel Shape Our Practice* (Grand Rapids: Baker, 2009), 228–229.
11. S. S. Curry, *Vocal and Literary Interpretation of the Bible* (New York: Macmillan, 1903), 132.

Empathy with the text is revealed through the voice and body—through what you sound like and look like as you read the ancient words. With a thousand and one subtle signs, we project our interior experience of the text, and when we do so, the listeners also experience the text. They are the last ring of iron in the chain, magnetized to the author's ideas and emotions through you. Although the audience's experience is vicarious, mediated through you, it is powerful nevertheless. As clergyman and rhetorician Hugh Blair said, "The only effectual method [of moving the listeners' emotions'] is to be moved yourself. . . . There is obviously a contagion among the passions."[12]

Some scientists describe this "contagion" in terms of "mirror neurons"—special nerve cells of the brain that prompt us to imitate the muscle tone and attitude of the person speaking to us. Mirror neurons were discovered in the mid-1990s and have become important in research on autism. People with autism have low levels of mirror neuron activity and thus are unable to read and imitate others' emotions. An article from the *Boston Globe* summarizes the research: "Scientists believe that the mirror neurons may help form the biological basis for empathy, and the penchant for imitation—the baby

---

12. Hugh Blair, *Lectures on Rhetoric and Belles Lettres* in Lester Thonssen and Craig Baird, *Speech Criticism: The Development of Standards for Rhetorical Appraisal* (New York: Roland, 1948), 364.

responding to the smile with a smile, the toddler clapping as the teacher claps."[13]

Knowledge of mirror neurons applies to oral interpretation of the Bible in this way: if you respond to the feelings of the text, and project that experience through your voice and body, particularly your face, the audience will also respond. Plato described the phenomenon with the analogy of the magnet. Blair described it as a "contagion among the passions," but they meant the same thing: empathy. Chapters 4 and 5 detail how we can project the text's ideas and feelings through delivery skills, but my point here is that we must first understand and feel what the author intends.

Here is a checklist to use as you prepare emotionally:

❑ Use the "magic if." This is the term of Stanislavski, the great Russian teacher of acting.[14] It simply says: *If* I were this character (say, the Prince of Denmark whose father had just died and whose mother had remarried his father's brother, and *if* I were of melancholy disposition, and *if* I suspected the new king of killing my father . . .) how would I behave? *If* you were Hagar, a concubine of Abraham for many years

---

13. Carey Goldberg, "We Feel Your Pain . . . And Your Happiness Too," *Boston Globe* (Dec. 12, 2005), C–1.

14. See Sonia Moore, *The Stanislavski System: The Professional Training of an Actor Digested from the Teachings of Konstantin S. Stanislavski* (New York: Penguin, 1965), 27–28.

who bore his heir, and *if* Abraham's wife forced you and the boy into the desert, and *if* you were near death, and *if* you were in despair . . . how would you tell the story of Genesis 21? Use the "magic if" to help you empathize.

❑ Pay special attention to sensory imagery. Much of the empathetic response the author intends is conveyed through the senses—sight, touch, taste, smell, and hearing. Notice the imagery of Job 4:12–16:

> Now a word was brought to me stealthily;
>> my ear received the whisper of it.
> Amid thoughts from visions of the night,
>> when deep sleep falls on men,
> dread came upon me, and trembling,
>> which made all my bones shake.
> A spirit glided past my face;
>> The hair of my flesh stood up.
> It stood still,
>> but I could not discern its appearance.
> A form was before my eyes;
>> there was silence, then I heard a voice
>
> . . . .

To respond to the moods the author intends, imagine the imagery.

❑ Read aloud. As stated in chapter 1, the experience of silent reading differs from that of oral reading. We use different areas of the brain for these activities. Both methods of preparation are valuable, but to feel emotions, use the ear. Robin Myers states,

> The preacher must first experience the text acoustically, allowing the words to create a circle that first echoes emotions and then elicits them. In the human drama of Scripture, fear has a sound, high and tight; so does longing; it is tired and drawn out. Awe and wonder have a sound too—it is a paradoxical sound, like trying to shout what can only be whispered. The *sound* of Scripture matters ultimately . . . because until he has heard what to feel, he cannot speak with enough feeling to be heard.[15]

❑ Listen to others read your passage. This can be almost as effective as speaking aloud. In both cases we experience the text more holistically than when reading silently. Here are some internet sites for listening to the Bible, some of which are free:

www.audioscriptures.org
www.Biblegateway.com/resources/audio
www.audiotreasure.com

---

15. Robin Myers, *With Ears to Hear: Preaching as Self-Persuasion* (Cleveland: Pilgrim, 1993), 43.

www.faithcomesbyhearing.com
www.listenersbible.com
www.scourby.com

Note: As you listen to these expert readers, be careful not to imitate them. Use them to help you imagine and empathize with the text, but be yourself.

❑ Space your preparation. Start a few days in advance, working on the reading in multiple sessions. The mind and emotions need time to acclimate to the landscape of the text. A few gifted readers may be able to identify with Hagar the first time they pick up the script, but most of us need time to adjust.

❑ Record yourself on video. This tool is our great schoolmaster, helping us perceive ourselves as the audience does. Most of us undersell the emotions of the text, tending toward an "aw-shucks" reading, but very few of us know that we undersell until we watch and hear ourselves. Most readers are surprised. They didn't know they were so deadpan. The pauses they used, which felt to them like an eternity of silence, were actually not long at all. The gestures they used, which felt strong and large, were actually half-hearted and vague. True, video can be painful to watch, but it is a God-given tool that can help us devote ourselves to public reading.

❏ Pray and practice. Review APCAT above. The better you prepare, the more confident you will feel.

6. Prepare your script.

We normally deliver the passage from the printed page, so prepare the page for easy reading. On occasion you may want to deliver the passage from memory, but that is usually not necessary and sometimes can undermine effectiveness if listeners pay more attention to your performance than to the Word. However, if the occasion warrants it, perhaps at a Christmas eve service of songs, dramatic readings, and Scripture, delivery from memory can enhance reception.

The suggestions below make the act of reading easy for you and effective for the listeners.

❏ Choose a translation for oral communication. In many churches this choice is made for you, but if you have freedom, choose intentionally rather than thoughtlessly. Choose something that fits the mood of the occasion, perhaps the New Living Translation for a casual service or the King James Version for a formal one. Choose something that communicates well for the ear such as the New International Version or the New King James Version. Some people find the New American Standard Version wooden (although laudably precise), and some find the King James Version archaic. The English Standard Version may be the best all-round translation, combining accuracy with readability.

I recommend reading from a translation rather than a paraphrase because our task as bridge builders is to help people connect with the actual message God communicated rather than an approximation of that message.

❑ Write and rehearse an introduction. The intro can be as brief as a simple announcement of the Scripture reference or as lengthy as a paragraph if you think people will need preparation before they can "enter" the world of the text. Remember that you have been working on your reading for several days—looking up words, noting context, imagining sensory information, and so forth—but the listeners will experience the text only once and only briefly. To help them engage quickly, both cognitively and emotively, you might need to explain a word, summarize the context, or briefly prepare them for the emotions they are about to experience. Here are a few examples of introductions:

> Our reading this morning is Psalm 32. Please turn to Psalm 32. [pause]

(Note: this brief introduction would be sufficient if the flow of the service has already been established. If people are already thinking some of the thoughts of the text and feeling some of its feelings, a longer introduction is superfluous.)

> Psalm 32, a psalm of David. Tradition says that King David wrote this poem after committing two great sins that marked his life—adultery with Bathsheba and murder of her husband, Uriah. For some time he lived in silence under the heavy hand of guilt, but then he finally confessed his sin, and God forgave. Now, in this psalm, he looks back on that experience and counsels us to learn from him. We too should confess our sins. Hear the Word of the Lord.

> Psalm 32 describes something each of us has experienced: guilt and forgiveness. David wrote this psalm when, as he says, God's hand was heavy upon him and he groaned in conviction. Do you know the feeling? But David also says that he acknowledged his sin, and God forgave. My prayer is that you would know that experience too. Listen to David teach us about guilt and forgiveness. Psalm 32.

If you expect the people to follow along in their Bibles as you read, give them time to find the text. Starting to read before listeners find the passage is one of the most common mistakes I see as I coach Scripture readers. Waiting in silence for folks to find the passage can be uncomfortable for the public reader, but it must be done. And when the congregation is occupied with finding the passage, they do not notice the silence. In a sense, time stands still for them, and they are not uncomfortable with the silence.

❏ Prepare a script that is easy to read. Hold the Bible as you read because this is a strong visual reminder to the congregation that you are speaking Someone Else's words, but you may want to type your passage on a separate sheet of paper and place it in your Bible. Make the act of reading easy, not laborious, by using a large font, extra line spacing, wide margins, colors, underlining, or any system of marks that are meaningful for you. Slash marks in particular are helpful to remind yourself of phrasing.

As electronic resources become more common, you may wonder if it is acceptable to read from an electronic tablet rather than a print version of the Bible. To decide, take into account the culture of the listeners. Some folks (and their number is shrinking) will be distracted by the use of a tablet. Make your decision as a servant to the listeners and as a steward of the Word. Do not make your decision solely on personal preference. If you do choose to read from an electronic device, learn how to mark the script with fonts, highlighting, and so forth.

My own marked script looks like this.

Genesis 22:1-2

After these things God **tested** Abraham and said to him,
   "Abraham"
And he said ————▶ "Here am I." //

He said, "Take you son / your only son Isaac / whom
you love / and go to the land of Moriah.
   And offer him there as a **burnt offering** on one of
   the mountains which I shall tell you. //

Figure 2.4: Marked Script

Slashes indicate a pause. Bold font indicates emphasis. Use of spacing and line lengths help with phrasing and subordination. The arrow indicates physical movement—taking a step forward.

7. Prepare your setting.

Remember that physical setting (time, place, acoustics, lighting, etc.) affects comprehension, so serve your listeners by preparing that setting. For example, make sure the audience can see and hear you. Plan where you will stand; determine how loud you need to be; consider how you will use eye contact for the shape of the room. What is the value of public reading if the audience cannot see and hear you? Furthermore, do the reading at a prominent moment of the service. Avoid what McLean and Bird call "blurring"—placing the reading at a moment that causes it to blend together with the other elements of the service.[16]

Here is a checklist to help you prepare the setting.

❑ If possible, have a friend listen to you from different positions in the sanctuary. Can your friend see and hear you? If not, what needs to be done? Is the light sufficient to illuminate your face—one of our primary channels of communication? Is the light sufficient for you to see your script easily? If more volume is needed, or clearer amplification, can you work with the person in charge of sound? Many readings fail because of issues involving sight and sound.

❑ Decide where you will stand and if you will move. In many cases this choice is made for you—tradition may dictate that you stand behind a lectern. But if you have freedom, use that freedom to enhance communication. In chapter 4 I'll talk more about "proxemics," the use of space for communication, and I demonstrate this on the DVD also.

❑ Determine where you will place your Bible/ script. Will you place it on the lectern or will you hold it? Make a choice that allows you to keep your face elevated rather than buried in

---

16. McLean and Bird, *Unleashing the Word*, 50.

the script. Position the script high enough so that your head does not bob up and down as your eyes shift from the page to the people. More on this in chapter 4 and on the DVD.

Conclusion

The table is set. You have prayed for God's blessing. You have studied the text so that you understand it and feel it. You have given attention to the mechanical aspects of reading, such as marking your script and resolving issues of sight and sound. You are almost ready to serve, but first you must invite the guests to the feast.

3

Inviting the Guests

"The only way to change culture is to create more of it. . . . Cultural change will only happen when something new displaces . . . existing culture in a very tangible way."

—Andy Crouch[1]

You have set the table by preparing yourself, your setting, and your script. Now you need to make sure someone is there to benefit from all of that preparation. This chapter is about establishing a culture that values oral interpretation of the Bible. To accomplish this, we first need to understand the values and practices that hinder that ministry.

---

1. Andy Crouch, *Culture Making* (Downers Grove, IL: InterVarsity, 2008), 66–67.

Hindrances to Public Reading

Like a farmer who no longer notices the smell of the pig pen, we can become so accustomed to poor reading that it no longer offends us. Last-minute, unpracticed, unpolished, mispronounced, mistimed, perfunctory and obligatory readings of the in-spired Word are the norm in some churches. These churches don't give them a second thought. Rather, when they hear the Word read with understanding and empathy, it sounds "weird." If I'm describing your culture, you will want to make changes slowly. The ears of people long attuned to "aw-shucks" and "ho-hum" will be sensitive to anything that smacks of the theatrical. And remember, practices stem from values. Ask yourself what values drive the practice of poor reading. To make lasting change in culture, you have to address values.

Another practice that hinders effective public reading is marginalizing it by giving it little time in the service. This practice may arise from the value of efficiency. If church leaders are hyper-conscious of the clock, with services never slipping past the sacred boundary of sixty minutes, they may cut "non-essentials" like Scripture reading. Leaders with this view often consider the sermon to be the most essential part of the service. They may be surprised to discover that when the Word is well read, the sermon can be shorter. Less time will be needed to explain the text and less time will be needed to create identification between the listen-ers and the text.

Changing a Culture

Imagine a culture where people enjoy hearing the Word, where they expect to "get something" from it, where it may even be the highlight of the service. Imagine a culture where, as the reader steps forward, listeners lean in, their hearts open, and their expectations rise. That's the kind of culture I want to be part of!

Here are four suggestions to help you create that kind of culture.[2] They are arranged in rough chronological sequence.

START WITH THE LEADERS. These people might be the pastoral staff, elders, or worship committee; or they might be less official but still influential people. Sometimes they are called "opinion leaders." Explain to them the theology of public reading, showing biblically why we are commanded to *devote* ourselves to this ancient practice. Do not rush this phase (or any of the phases below) because cultural change cannot be mandated top-down. It is strongest when it arises from below and from within.

You might want to begin by having the leaders read the first chapters of this book. As I write, I am in the midst of my own attempt to influence culture. To help my church catch the vision of effective public reading, I first took a proposal to

---

2. To go deeper on how to change a culture, see Andy Crouch, *Culture Making*, and Robert Lewis, Wayne Cordeiro, and Warren Bird, *Culture Shift: Transforming Your Church from the Inside Out* (Hoboken, NJ: Jossey-Bass, 2005).

the committee that oversees our worship services. I presented the material from chapter 1 and answered their questions. Our conversation helped them develop a desire for a new way of doing things, and it also showed me issues I had not thought about. The leaders you talk to will want concrete examples and details of what you have in mind: Who will do the reading? How much time will be devoted to it? And so forth. You might not have answers to all their questions, and that's okay because the vision will grow best if it arises from the roots. Brainstorming helps everyone shape and own the vision.

CAST VISION TO THE CONGREGATION. This phase will probably be less dialogic than the first, but it will be most effective if it is more than pure monologue. Preach and teach on the subject of worship. Show how Scripture reading is a necessary component of "covenant renewal." Theologian John Davis recommends preaching on two portions of Scripture that are especially pertinent: Exodus 19–24 and Hebrews 12:18–29. In the first passage God forms a covenant with his chosen people at Mount Sinai and illustrates many of the elements of an effective worship service: the call to assemble, God's presence, God speaking his words, and his people responding with promises of obedience. This passage shows that the basic pattern of worship is revelation-response.[3]

---

3. John Jefferson Davis, *Worship and the Reality of God: An*

START A READING TEAM. This is the phase I am in with my church. I invited five people who have background in acting or public speaking. I did not hold auditions, although I may do so in the future, because I wanted to avoid any association with theatrics. The five readers are already convinced that we should increase the quantity and quality of our reading, so at our first meeting I spent just a few minutes casting vision. We then spent the majority of our time coaching each other. Knowing that it is a fearful thing to fall into the hands of a live audience, I volunteered to be the first one to receive coaching. I read a passage and then took suggestions such as "slow down" or "try adding a pause here." This process continued for fifteen or twenty minutes. I tried to model openness and I expressed appreciation for the help they gave. This set the tone for future coaching sessions. Eventually this team will try some of the creative methods described in chapters 6 and 7, but for now we are taking it slow. We will also watch recordings of professional readers to learn from them. The goal is to coach and equip the team as they devote themselves to the public reading.

CREATE SOMETHING BETTER. As Andy Crouch states, "Cultural change will only happen when something new displaces . . . existing culture in a

---

Evangelical Theology of Real Presence (Downers Grove, IL: InterVarsity, 2010), 174.

very tangible way."[4] In this process of displacing, once again, don't move too fast. If your church is in a rut of homiletical throat-clearing, you may want to take the small step of simply adding an "extra" reading, something related to the sermon but not the exact text that will be expounded. If your church is in a rut of ho-hum, you might play a recording of a professional for that Sunday's reading. Or better—you might bring in a professional such as Hunter Barnes.[5] Part of my attempt to form a new culture includes that very thing. We brought Hunter to my church to recite the entire book of Mark. There was no sermon on that Sunday, just the water, milk, and bread of the Word. It helped people experience the power of the Bible.

The table is set and the guests have been invited. It is time to serve the meal!

---

4. *Culture Making*, 66–68.
5. See http://www.imaginetheword.com.

4

Serving the Meal

(Communicating Through What We Look Like)

Manner is not everything. Still, if you have gathered good matter, it is a pity to convey it meanly; a king should not ride in a dustcart.

—Charles Spurgeon[1]

Let the gesture tally with the words, and be a sort of running commentary and practical exegesis upon what you are saying.

—Charles Spurgeon[2]

The face is what is most expressive. . . . It is often equivalent in expressiveness to what can be said in many words.

—Quintilian[3]

Drink to me only with thine eyes, / And I will pledge with mine.

—Ben Jonson

1. C. H. Spurgeon, *Lectures to My Students*, Vol. 1 (1875, rpt. Grand Rapids: Baker, 1977), 143.
2. Spurgeon, *Lectures to My Students*, Vol. 2, 115.
3. In Bryan Chapell, *Christ-Centered Worship*, 231.

Oral interpreters "serve the meal" by reading well. They use their voices and bodies—what they sound like and look like—to make the words come alive. Unlike preachers who stand between the text and the audience by expounding on what is written, oral interpreters do not add commentary. They "merely" read. Their exposition comes through how they say the words of the Bible. Of course, "merely" reading is not simple, and that is why you're reading this book!

An adage of communication states, "You cannot not communicate." That is, all of our behaviors, verbal and non verbal, convey a message. There is no neutral stance, facial expression, or gesture. There is no communication vacuum. A rigid posture carries its own message, as does a relaxed posture. A knit brow implies a message, as does a raised brow. You may say, "But I didn't intend to communicate anything with my facial expression. That's just the way I look!" That may well be true, but consider two other perspectives.

First, in some ways it doesn't matter what you intended. Listeners instinctively try to "decode" non verbal cues from the speaker's face, eyes, hands, posture, and so forth. Rightly or wrongly, all of us belong to the LNVD (i.e., the League of Non-Verbal Decoders). Much of this decoding occurs below the level of consciousness (remember the discussion of "empathy" in chapter 2), but it occurs nevertheless. That is the dynamic behind the adage, "You cannot not communicate." All of us get "impressions" of speakers—"she seemed distracted" or "he's so sincere"—but often we cannot identify the reason for those impressions. Thus, you cannot not communicate. For public reading, this means that all actions of the body and nuances of the voice contribute to the listeners' experience of the text.

Second, remember Jesus' words, "Out of the heart, the mouth speaks." From an angry heart come angry words. From a courageous heart come bold words. The heart is a word factory, and that truth can be extended to non verbal communication as well as verbal. Out of the heart, the body behaves. Out of the heart, the brow is knit, the arms are crossed, the hands are open, or the eyes are averted. To be sure, numerous heart conditions could lie behind the crossed arms, but my point here (and I think it is Jesus' point too) is that a subterranean stream of belief and emotion percolates into exterior behavior. That is why listeners instinctively trust the non-verbal channel. That is why all of us belong to the LNVD. That is why you cannot not communicate. As stated previously, sixty-five percent of all "social meaning" and ninety-three percent of "emotional meaning" is communicated through the non verbal channel.[4]

---

4. Randall P. Harrison, "Nonverbal Communication: Exploration into Time, Space, Action, and Object," *Dimensions in Communication*, eds. James H. Campbell and Hal W. Hepler (Belmont, CA: Wadsworth, 1965), 161; and Albert Mehrabian, *Silent Messages* (Belmont, CA: Wadsworth, 1971), 77.

The nature of a relationship (romance, mentoring, business, etc.) and the state of the affections (happiness, sadness, compassion, etc.) are conveyed by the tone of voice and disposition of the body.

This chapter and the next examine our two channels of communication: our voices and bodies—what we sound like and what we look like. We begin with what we look like, our bodily action. Unfortunately, Scripture readers often are oblivious to the most obvious and negative form of bodily action, a menagerie of behaviors I call "distracting mannerisms."

Distracting Mannerisms

We've all seen it—hands that twitch, feet that rock, a head that bobs like a chicken hunting grasshoppers. I had a professor in college who would straighten his necktie an average of twenty times per class. Yes, I kept count. I was one of those easily distracted students. Spurgeon's description fit me: "The majority of hearers fix their eyes mainly upon . . . little oddities and absurdities of mode and gesture."[5]

We all have distracting mannerisms, but few of us are aware of our own. After my first speech, a junior high oration as part of an induction ceremony in which the speakers wore robes, my classmates informed me of my own contribution to the catalog of distracting mannerisms. They called it

---

5. *Lectures to My Students*, Vol. 2, 96.

"robe-fwapping." While my speech lumbered for all of sixty seconds, and while I made graceful gestures with my right hand, my left hand kept fwapping my robe. I must have fiddled and wiped and slapped that robe twenty times in sixty seconds, but I never knew I was doing it.

To overcome distracting mannerisms we have to become aware of them and move through these stages:

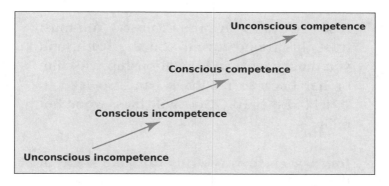

Figure 4.1: Process of Gaining Awareness and Skill

In the first stage of this process we are not aware that we are twitching, rocking, or bobbing or fwapping.

The second stage is the most painful because we become aware of our failings. I still remember my embarrassment after the fwapping incident. But take heart! Much of the art of effective reading is the elimination of poor habits, which is impossible without stage two. We must become aware. Like a hunter scanning for rabbits in the autumn brush, you have to see your game before taking aim.

Here are three ways to become aware of your distracting mannerisms:

WATCH YOURSELF ON VIDEO. Ouch! But there is no better schoolmaster to improve delivery. We must "get outside" of ourselves to see our reading as the audience does.

ASK A FRIEND TO GIVE YOU FEEDBACK. You must trust this friend to tell you the truth, and you must have a solid relationship with him or her because feedback can also lead to "ouch!" Be brave; God will bless your humility.

JOIN A READING TEAM. This can take some of the "ouch" out of feedback as each member of the team volunteers to receive coaching.

The third stage is both awkward and invigorating: awkward because you have to consciously control your bobbing head, but invigorating because you are controlling it! This is the stage where I do most of my coaching. I give readers suggestions such as these: "Maintain eye contact longer on verse three" or "Before you begin, take a full breath and relax your shoulders." We work on skills like these and see rapid improvement.

The final stage is bliss. Like a professional basketball player who no longer has to think about form but "merely" drives to the hoop and scores, your hard work has paid off. When the fire of the Word blazes in your heart and you express it without awkward self-consciousness, then the hearts of the listeners catch fire too.

Although distracting mannerisms can occur with any of the components of bodily action (as well as with the use of the voice), they often adhere to gestures.

Gestures

The term "gesture" usually refers to movements of the hands, but it is actually broader than that. Charlotte Lee defines the term as "any clearly discernable movement which helps express or emphasize an idea."[6] This includes obvious gestures such as raising and lowering the hands, as when a reader says "Welcome" or "Stop"; pointing, as when the reader says "It's over there"; and folding the arms to show anger or a sudden chill. But gesturing also involves other parts of the body, such as the head when a reader lifts her eyes and face, and the shoulders as when we shrug or cringe.

Like every other aspect of non verbal communication, gesturing must be the result of the reader's response to the text. In other words, gesturing must be sincere, not "play-acting." In years past,

---

6. *Oral Reading of the Scriptures* (Boston: Houghton Mifflin, 1974), 21.

under the influence of the "Elocution" movement, orators and readers used sweeping gestures and melodramatic stances. This technique, by today's standards, looks artificial and mechanical. The influence of the Elocutionists extended even into the twentieth century and can be seen in the pantomimic acting style of silent movies. Here are some diagrams from an 1806 Elocutionist textbook.[7]

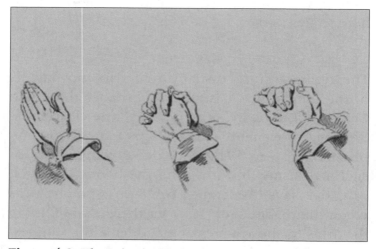

Figure 4.2: Elocutionist Training—Use of the Hands

---

7. The textbook is Gilbert Austin's *Chironomia* (1806). The diagrams are accessible at http://www.google.com/search?tbm=i sch&hl=en&source=hp&biw=1024&bih=667&q=elocutionist+ diagrams&gbv=2&oq=elocutionist+diagrams&aq=f&aqi=&aql =&gs_sm=e&gs_upl=70l1l0739l0l10957l23l23l1l16l16l0l222l9 70l1.2.3l6l0#hl=en&gbv=2&tbm=isch&sa=X&ei=7q5nTvmdKM fqgQfO2t3oDA&ved=0CDsQvwUoAQ&q=austin+chironomia &spell=1&bav=on.2,or.r_gc.r_pw.&fp=d1322a9eb53a80d3&biw =1024&bih=667

Figure 4.3: Elocutionist Training—Gestures

The Elocutionists tried to create a scientific system of gesture that linked each emotion to one particular gesture. This style is now, thankfully, passé. Don't do it!

On the other hand, remember that public communication is different from interpersonal communication. When reading to a group of fifty or five hundred, we must project, and projection includes the use of the body as well as the voice. When you watch yourself on video you may find, as most readers do, that your gestures are neither energetic nor definite. They would work fine for interpersonal communication, but they appear indistinct and half-

75

hearted in public reading, poorly conveying ideas and feelings.

Another key to effective gesturing is variety. Too often we use a single habitual movement to convey varied emotions such as happiness, sadness, anger, entreaty, welcome, rejection, thanks, refusal, doubt, agreement, confusion, or certainty. The Scripture reader who is comfortable with only one or two gestures is like a pitcher who has only a fastball.

Think of what can be done with flexible and energetic gestures. The head and shoulders can convey weariness, pride, resignation, or curiosity. An open hand can convey taking, receiving, inviting, or surrendering. A clenched fist can convey anger, power, or fear. A hand turned on its side can divide a room or focus a proposition as when the speaker says "Come now, let us reason together, says the Lord." A hand with palm turned down can convey rejection or control, and a raised index finger can announce or warn. Add a change up, slider, and curveball to your delivery and you'll help the team win more often.

Holding the Bible or standing behind a pulpit limits gestures but does not have to eliminate them. Keep one hand under the Bible, if you are holding it, and place the other one on top of it using your finger tips to mark your place. From that stance, you can gesture occasionally with the top hand, and those gestures can employ all the variety suggested above. If the Bible is resting on the pulpit, you have the option of using both hands, but your gestures will have to be higher than usual to be seen.

Choose a gesture appropriate to the idea or emotion you have discovered while studying the text (see chapter 2). Practice until it is natural, moving from conscious to unconscious competence, and then express with freedom and energy. There is no such thing as a right or wrong gesture (my apologies to any Elocutionists who may be reading this), just one that is effective or ineffective in our task as bridge builders to help listeners understand and feel the text.

Posture

Closely related to gesturing is posture and stance. This form of bodily action is subtle and rarely noticed by the audience unless it is poor. The old advice to "throw your shoulders back" like an Army recruit is actually off target. The key to good posture relates more to the ribs than to the shoulders. If you raise your rib cage out of your waist, "displaying" your sternum, you can relax your shoulders. They will naturally fall into correct alignment. Stand tall, asking God for appropriate confidence, eager to share the good news of the Word. Readers sometimes lean forward from the waist to express urgency, and this can be effective if used sparingly, but I often see it done with unconscious incompetence, and it looks melodramatic.

How might you use posture to help express these statements?

"I lift up my eyes to the hills." (Ps.121:1)

"I, Nebuchadnezzar, was at ease in my house and prospering in my palace. I saw a dream that made me afraid. As I lay in bed the fancies and the visions of my head alarmed me." (Dan.4:4–5)

"The women sang to one another as they celebrated,

> 'Saul has struck down his thousands,
>> and David his ten thousands.'

And Saul was very angry, and this saying displeased him. He said, "They have ascribed to David ten thousands and to me they have ascribed thousands, and what more can he have but the kingdom?' and Saul eyed David from that day on." (1 Sam.18:7–9)

Some Scripture readers deliver the text while seated, using a stool or table. This stance is becoming more common in North America as churches migrate toward a casual style, but even in those churches the choice to sit still calls for discernment. If your church culture "allows" it, sitting can be used effectively for a variety of purposes, conveying things like casualness and contemplation, or setting an atmosphere of invitation and dialogue, but if your culture does not "allow" it, do not distract attention from the Word by calling attention to self. As communication scholar Charles Bartow says, "Our [non-verbal] behavior . . . should not draw attention to itself and so become the object of our listeners' scorn or praise, fascination or disinterest."[8] Remember, there is no "right" and "wrong" in matters of delivery, just helpful and unhelpful. Servants seek to help.

Movement

"Movement" refers to walking—taking steps. Scripture readers normally do little of this, especially if they are behind a pulpit or lectern or at a stationary microphone, but sometimes the culture and technology permit movement. If you choose to move, do so purposefully. Don't shamble. Movement can work well to help communicate these aspects of your text:

- Transitions. As your text progresses from one major idea to another, or even one dominant mood to another, you can help the listeners make that journey by taking a few lateral steps. This use of movement works well when coupled with a pause.

- Emphasis. If the author of your text stresses an

---

8. *The Preaching Moment: A Guide to Sermon Delivery* (Nashville: Abingdon, 1980), 93.

idea or reaches an emotional climax, stepping toward listeners can place that moment in the spot light, so to speak.

- De-emphasis. This is the opposite of the point above. After the climax, when the listeners need a moment to ponder or process what they have heard, after you have walked toward them, you might pause and return to your original location.

Without sharing in the "sins" of the Elocutionists, with their mandated prescriptions, here is an example of where movement might help you serve the meal of Psalm 77. The arrows indicate direction of movement.

Psalm 77

I cry aloud to God,
>Aloud to God, and he will hear me.
In the day of my trouble I see the Lord;
>In the night my hand is stretched out
>without wearying;
>My soul refuses to be comforted.

[*The psalm continues for the next 7 verses to lament, but then in verse 10 a major shift of idea and emotion occurs. At the beginning of verse 9 I take a few steps laterally.*]

Then I said, I will appeal to this,

to the years of the right hand of the
Most High.
I will remember the deeds of the Lord,
Yes, I will remember your wonders of
old.

[The psalmist proceeds to remember God's mighty acts of the past, in particular the Exodus, reaching a vivid climax in verse 18. At that point, I take a step towards the audience.]

The crash of your thunder was in the
whirlwind;
your lightnings lighted up the world;
the earth trembled and shook.

[Verses 19 and 20 conclude by briefly showing the people of Israel safely through the Sea, continuing their journey to the Promised Land. You might pause and move back to your original position.]

You led your people like a flock
by the hand of Moses and Aaron.

One other word about movement: When you walk to the pulpit (or other place of reading) do so with purpose and energy. As soon as the audience becomes aware of you, you start communicating with them, so you'll want to convey confidence, preparedness, and alacrity. In a sense, your reading begins and ends in your seat.

Facial Expression

When interpreting a speaker's meaning, and even more so when evaluating a speaker's emotional state, listeners look at the face. In his classic studies from the 1960s, psychologist Albert Mehrabian concluded that when speakers conveyed their feelings in an ambiguous way, that is, when their words did not seem to match their "delivery," listeners interpreted the speaker's feelings based on facial expression and tone of voice more than words.[9]

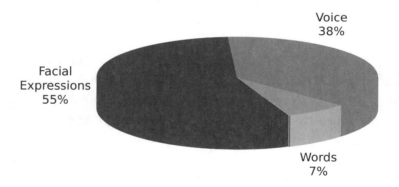

Figure 8: Listeners Rely on the Face to Decipher Emotions

---

9. Albert Mehrabian, "Communication Without Words," *Psychology Today* 2 (Sept. 1968), 53.

Listeners intuitively trust the face. This is because speakers can easily deceive with words, and almost as easily deceive with gestures, but they find it much more difficult to deceive with their faces. A relatively unadulterated stream flows from the heart through the face. Out of the heart the face "speaks." Perhaps this is because we are not particularly aware of our faces. We do not see them, so we are less likely to manipulate them. Another reason listeners trust facial expression is because six core expressions seem to be universal: happiness, sadness, anger, surprise, fear, and disgust. With remarkable consistency, people from all over the world do the same thing with their faces when feeling those emotions. Even more remarkably, blind-deaf babies do too. The six core facial expressions are not taught, as is most of our nonverbal communication, although socialization *does* teach us when and where to allow certain expressions.[10]

Facial expression is important to effective communication because listeners trust it. However, it is very difficult to coach facial expression. Self-conscious manipulation of the lips and eyebrows

---

10. See Mark L. Knapp and Judith A. Hall, *Nonverbal Communication in Human Interaction*, 3rd ed. (New York: Holt, Rinehart and Winston, 1992); Paul Ekman and W. V. Friesen, *Unmasking the Face* (Englewood Cliffs, NJ: Prentice-Hall, 1975); and Barry S. Brummett, Linda L. Putnam, and Richard E. Crable, *Principles of Human Communication*, 2nd ed., (Dubuque, IA: Kendall/Hunt, 1984), 78–9.

looks "canned," so the only sure way to use the powerful and trusted channel of the face is to truly feel the feelings the text has captured. Remember the discussion of "empathy" in chapter 2. There is a "contagion among the passions," but *you* have to be infected first! Or, as Plato might say, you have to be magnetized before the lodestone can draw the listeners up.

One aspect of facial expression that *can* be coached is projection. Most of us are deadpanned when we read. We think we are being more expressive than we actually are as we dwell in unconscious incompetence (again, video recording is the great schoolmaster).

When you stand up to read, "Bless the Lord, oh my soul, and all that is within me, bless his holy name" (Ps. 103:1), smile and project your sincere worship of our great God. When you read, "But sexual immorality and all impurity or covetousness must not even be named among you" (Eph. 5:3), let the stern command resonate in your heart and transfer naturally to your face. When you read how the sons of Jacob scorned Joseph, "Here comes this dreamer" (Gen. 37:19), ignite your imagination and engage your face. Rather than explaining to the listeners the "social meaning" the brothers intended, show it to them with your face. Project.

Eye contact

With the eyes we maintain attention, monitor feedback, compensate for physical distance, and signal the nature of a relationship. With the eyes we comfort, encourage, warn, scold, question, refuse, and engage. The eyes reveal the heart, just as the face does, so that the proverb says, "The eyes are the window of the soul." Infants intuitively look into their mother's eyes, and animals intuitively look at the eyes of their master or quarry. Picture a sheep dog rounding up sheep.

To see eye contact at work in Scripture, recall the profound communication that took place between our Lord and Peter, a communication with no words: "The Lord turned and looked straight at Peter. Peter remembered . . . went outside and wept bitterly" (Luke 22:61–62).

To minister the Word, use your eyes. Most platform communication demands nearly unbroken eye contact with the audience, but when *reading* in public, you will need to look down at times. That is fine. The audience knows you are reading, so there is no need to pretend otherwise. However, the audience still wants to see your eyes. They depend on your eyes to help them understand and imagine the content of the passage. For effective use of eye contact, try to achieve a fifty-fifty ratio. That is, your eyes should relate to the audience as much as they do to the page. This is difficult to do, so here are some tips. (Remember, this material is illustrated on the DVD).

- Approach the pulpit with your Bible closed and keep it closed throughout the introduction;

then pause, look down, open the Bible, look up, and begin.

- Practice so that you can grasp a sentence with one glance.

- Create a script with large font, and mark it. (See chapter 2.)

- Hold your script high, as if you were in the choir holding your music. If you are using a lectern, adjust the height.

- Look into the eyes of the listeners. Don't just scan. Pause for a second or two with individuals. If your audience is large, make eye contact with at least one person in each section of the room—someone in the left portion of the balcony, someone in the back right, someone in the center, and so forth. Because public reading is a communal event, everyone in the section will feel that you are communicating with them.

Proxemics

"Proxemics" refers to the use of space. I'll say more about this in coming chapters as we "add some spice" to the meal, and I've already touched on the subject in the section on movement, so this is just a reminder that where we position ourselves sends its own message. Delivering the reading from the midst of the congregation, or from the balcony, or seated on the edge of the platform sends a message. Standing behind a large pulpit sends a message of authority and distance, just as standing on stage with no pulpit or lectern sends a message of openness and freedom. As stated above, there is no "right" and "wrong" in matters of delivery, but as servants we are looking for the best way to serve the feast of the Word. What you look like is crucial to effective public reading, as is what you sound like, the topic of the next chapter.

5

—

Serving the Meal

(Communicating with the Voice)

The church is always trying to get other people
to reform; it might not be a bad idea to reform
itself a little, by way of example . . . . The average
clergyman could not fire into his congregation
with a shotgun and hit a worse reader than himself,
unless that weapon scattered shamefully. I am not
meaning to be flippant and irreverent, I am only
meaning to be truthful. The average clergyman, in
all countries and of all denominations, is a very
bad reader.

—Mark Twain[1]

---

1. *A Tramp Abroad*, vol. 2 (Hartford: American, 1880), 92. In Robert G. Jacks, *Getting the Word Across: Speech Communication
for Pastors and Lay Leaders* (Grand Rapids: Eerdmans, 1995),
11.

> To read well is a rare accomplishment. It is much more common to excel in singing, or in public speaking. Good preachers are numerous, compared with good readers.
>
> —John Broadus[2]

M OST OF THE work of serving the meal is done with the voice. The art of *oral interpretation* earns its designation when we take up the subject of the voice because how we use our voices is an act of exegesis.

For example, when Jesus exhorted Peter with a simple three-word sentence, "Feed my sheep," which word do you think Jesus emphasized? How would you interpret Jesus' words?

If your study of the passage has convinced you that Jesus was stressing the need to nourish the sheep, you would say, "*Feed* my sheep."

If your study revealed that Jesus was affirming his love for the sheep, and that he was transferring his role as shepherd to Peter, you would say, "Feed *my* sheep."

Or if you believe that Jesus was contrasting

---

2. John Broadus, *On the Preparation and Delivery of Sermons*, ed. Jesse B. Weatherspoon (London: Hodder and Stoughton, 1944), 479.

sheep (those who followed him) with goats (those who had rejected him), you would say, "Feed my *sheep*."

We convey meaning and mood by how we say printed words. Every instance of communication contains both denotative and connotative meanings, and the reader's voice is the primary tool for getting those meanings across.

I've divided this chapter into six parts for the six "P's" of effective use of the voice.

Projection

"Projection" means turning up the intensity of your communication so that it carries. Projection is like the master control on an audio board that turns up all the components at once.

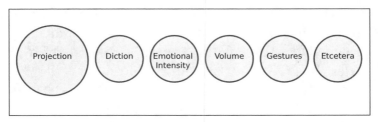

Figure 5.1: Projection

Notice that volume is one of the components, but it is not the most important one. Diction is most important. You can speak quite softly, even in a whisper, and be understood in the last row of the balcony if you articulate your consonants with energy and precision. This is difficult for beginners to grasp because they naively assume that the level of projection used in interpersonal communication is sufficient for public communication. As stated previously, however, the two are not the same. An "audience" seated next to you can read your face and eyes. But an audience twenty feet or twenty yards away cannot easily read your body language and may not be able to distinguish your "t's" from your "d's" and your "s's" from your "z's." Turning up volume without sharpening diction drowns the listeners in a tidal wave of undifferentiated sound.

The only way to become comfortable with the extra demands of crisp diction is to practice under the watchful ear and eye of a coach. You could coach yourself with audio and video recording, but it is more helpful to have a friend sit in the last row of the balcony and let you know how you are coming across. Most Scripture readers are surprised that they have to "overdo" their diction in order to serve the Word effectively.

You may say, "But we use microphones! There is no need for the orotund tones of the Elocutionists." You are right. But remember that the microphone simply magnifies what you give it. Amplified mush is still mush. If you give the microphone a bog of unarticulated vowel sounds, it cannot save you. So, spit out your consonants! "T" is not "d." "Z" is not "s."

Another component of projection, almost a second master switch, is what Spurgeon called "earnestness."[3] I've labeled this "emotional intensity" in the figure above. If you have immersed yourself in the text so that you see the scene and feel the feelings, and if you care about those who sit before you, your reading will have the same energy you use in "earnest conversation."[4] Listen to two animated Red Sox fans recount last night's game against the Yankees, and you will hear earnest conversation.

To project your voice without strain, shift the "center of emotion" from the throat and jaw to the epigastric region (mid-stomach, just below your solar plexus and above your belt). Speakers who become hoarse are using their throats rather than the epigastric muscles to convey intensity. To test yourself, read this sentence with earnestness and see where you tense up: "O my son Absalom, my son, my son, Absalom! Would I had died instead of you. O Absalom, my son, my son!" (2 Sam.18:33). If your throat and jaw are tight, transfer the "center of emotion" to your gut and express it from there. That is the region of your body that powers the lungs. When you inhale, the diaphragm tenses, flattening downward, thus increasing the volume of the lungs so that air rushes in from atmospheric pressure. When you

3. C. H. Spurgeon, *Lectures to My Students*, vol. 1 (1875, rpt. Grand Rapids: Baker, 1977), 120.

4. This is Spurgeon's phrase. Stephen H. Webb calls it "high conversation." *The Divine Voice: Christian Proclamation and the Theology of Sound* (Grand Rapids: Brazos, 2004), 210.

exhale, the diaphragm relaxes and the epigastric muscles push the air through the vocal folds. This is hard to describe in writing (as is most of the art of oral interpretation), so take a look at the DVD.

Projection requires full body involvement. Stand tall, make your gestures full and energetic, and use overt (but not "canned") facial expression. The voice follows the body. Above the control board of a radio station where I worked, the station manager had placed a sign to remind all announcers: "Put a smile in your voice." People can hear a smile as well as see one. But it is impossible to smile in your voice if the whole body is not also smiling. So rev up your body and the voice will come along for the ride. Empathy (the heart) controls the body and the body controls the voice. All of it is wired to the master control called "projection."

Phrasing

Read idea by idea, not word by word. This means that you will emphasize key words and phrases, and just as importantly, you will *subordinate* words and phrases of secondary importance. The human ear needs variety. We cannot process ideas presented in a monotone, mono-rate, or mono--volume. The drone of a fan soon becomes background noise. Giving equal emphasis to every word sounds like a schoolboy reciting his lesson:

The / Lord / is / my / shepherd / I / shall / not / want / he / makes / me / lie / down . . .

When every word receives equal emphasis, the meaning will be missing even though the words are correct.

The question then arises: "How do I know what to emphasize and what to subordinate?" Answer: study. Understand the author's intention. In general, we should emphasize key ideas, new ideas, and contrasting ideas. For example, in the sentence above from Psalm 23, the key image is that God is a *shepherd*. The next phrase extends that idea by showing its implications: David shall *not want*. Subordinate unimportant words like "the," "is," and "shall." The word "the" will hardly even be vocalized, just as you subordinate the word when you say, "I pledge allegiance to the flag." (Once again, I recommend the DVD so that you can hear these techniques rather than simply read about them.) In Psalm 23 you will have to make a decision on the word "my." It may be crucial enough to the meaning and emotion of the psalm that you will emphasize it.

How does the thought progress in this verse? Say it out loud to bring out the progression.

> "Peace I leave with you; my peace I give you. Not as the world gives do I give to you." (John 14:27).

Punctuation marks often help with vocal phrasing, but not always. Sometimes they get in the way. In this passage, pausing at each comma breaks up the sense.

And he took bread, and when he had given thanks, he broke it and gave it to them, saying, "This is my body, which is given for you." (Luke 22:19)

Rather than pausing at each comma, I recommend:

And he took bread, / and when he had given thanks, he broke it and gave it to them, / saying, "This is my body, which is given for you."

For in-depth training on phrasing, find a copy of *How to Speak the Written Word*[5] by Nedra Newkirk Lamar, the queen of this science. Her organization, the Institute of Analytical Reading, trains public readers, including broadcasters, Scripture readers, lawyers, and actors.

Pause

The pause may be the most effective form of vocal emphasis. When we break the cadence of speech with silence, the ear is magnetized to what follows. As Spurgeon said, "A very useful help in securing attention is *a pause.* Pull up short every now and then, and the passengers on your coach will wake up."[6]

---

5. *How to Speak the Written Word: A Guide to Effective Public Reading* (Westwood, NJ: Revell, 1949). Chapter 6 is about Bible reading in particular. See the website: www.analyticalreading. org.

6. *Lectures to My Students*, vol. 1, 148.

Besides gaining attention, the pause encourages mental interaction, creates mystery, shows respect for the audience or event, and conveys emotion. It is supremely valuable in building a bridge from the ancient text to the modern listeners, helping listeners understand and feel the force of God's Word. Homiletician Webb Garrison said,

> Silence—supplemented by gesture and changed in tone and force—has to serve as comma, period, question mark, exclamation point, colon, dash and every other punctuation device. Failure to use silence produces oral communication that is like an ancient Hebrew scroll—plenty of ideas, but all crowded together, rolling on and on with majestic and incomprehensible unconcern.[7]

When used strategically, the pause is a cessation of sound, not thought. We communicate in silence.

Even though the pause has such power, novice readers are hesitant to use it. They are uncomfortable with silence. They need to learn that the pause always seems longer to the speaker than to the congregation. As readers we must learn to perceive ourselves the way others perceive us. The best ways to do that, once again, are with video/audio recording or the feedback of a coach. Add some judicious

---

7. Webb B. Garrison, *The Preacher and His Audience* (Grand Rapids: Revell, 1951), 118.

silence to your reading and you will rivet hearts and minds.

Pace

Closely related to pause is "pace," or rate of speech. Most North Americans speak about 150 words per minute. That rate probably slows when doing public speaking and may slow even more when doing public reading. The reason is that written communication is more condensed and less redundant than oral communication, and when written language is changed to sound, listeners need time to grasp the condensed thought. This is especially true with closely reasoned passages, such as those in the book of Romans, or with the emotive and metaphorical language of lyric poetry, such as psalms.

The use of a particular rate of speech is one of the qualities that marks your personal speaking style. Be yourself. There is no need to strive for a certain number of words per minute unless you are stultifying in your slowness or incomprehensible in your speed. The key to effective communication, in terms of pace, is to make sure you have variety. Be like New England weather—sun and sleet, rain and drought—anything but fog. Intoning at a steady rate produces fog. A steady rate is the primary vocal faux pas. It makes public reading sound like a canned recitation rather than personal, delivering only words, not heart and soul.

Pitch

Just as the human ear craves variety of pace, so it craves variety of pitch. No one likes a monotone. Our brains quickly drive the droning of a fluorescent light into the far reaches of consciousness lest we go crazy! The key to a lively, interesting voice, once again, is variety. Rising in pitch at the end of statement implies uncertainty or surprise, just as dropping the pitch implies conviction, boredom, or disappointment. Varying the pitch in the middle of a sentence, as with the Greek circumflex accent, carries its own connotations, as when we say "Wait a minute" implying, "Something fishy is going on here." Try using pitch to convey various meanings from the same sentence: "You don't mean that, do you?"

- (Accusing)—end on a downward thump.

- (Uncertain)—end on an upward, almost suspended note.

- (Hopeful and assuring)—use an inverted circumflex pattern starting high, dropping low, and ending high again, as if to say, "I'm sure you don't mean that."

Punch

"Punch" refers to loudness, the number of decibels the voice produces. It is sometimes called "force." This is the easiest type of vocal emphasis and thus is overused. Using punch five times on nine words is the vocal equivalent of the boy who cried wolf. After a while your words will fall on deaf ears:

> The **LORD** is **MY SHEPHERD**. I shall **NOT** want.

Listeners feel overwhelmed and distrustful of such vocal hyperbole. Save punch for a few choice moments when the text warrants it. How might you use force on this passage?

> He makes wars cease to the end of the earth;
> he breaks the bow and shatters the spear;
> he burns the chariots with fire.

> Be still, and know that I am God. (Ps. 46:9–10)

Instinctively, you probably dropped the decibels on the last line, and the contrast emphasized that line even better than increasing the decibels. Learn from that: dropping the volume often rivets attention. But the key to effective use of punch is variety. Just as mono-pace, and mono-pitch are deadly to communication, so is mono-force.

Putting it all together

In this chapter I've separated the P's, but in reality we use multiple techniques every time we speak. For example, if you dropped the decibels on the line, "Be still, and know that I am God," you almost certainly slowed the pace and lowered the pitch.

Experiment with your voice on a single syllable: "Oh." Convey these emotions:

- Pity (You have received news that your friend has not been accepted into grad school.)

- Disbelief (That's impossible! Surely they would accept you into their graduate program.)

- Anger (They haven't accepted you just because you are over fifty. How outrageous!)

- Delight (You've been accepted!)

- Wariness (Your friend is now going to ask you for a loan so he or she can pay for grad school.)

Here are some exercises from Jana Childers' *Performing the Word*.[8] Experiment with the six P's to convey the meaning in parentheses. Remember that punch is easiest to use. There is nothing wrong with it, but also see if you can convey the meaning with the other techniques.

- *I* never said she stole my purse. (Maybe someone else said it.)

---

8. Jana M. Childers, *Performing the Word: Preaching as Theatre* (Nashville: Abingdon, 1998), 85.

- I *never* said she stole my purse. (I didn't say it before, and I'm not saying it now.)

- I never *said* she stole my purse. (Maybe I implied it.)

- I never said *she* stole my purse. (It was someone else altogether.)

- I never said she *stole* my purse. (Now that I think of it, she might have just borrowed it.)

- I never said she stole *my* purse. (But she did steal someone else's!)

- I never said she stole my *purse*. (It was my wallet I was complaining about.)

In these exercises we're adding "word color" to bring out the emotional and relational connotations of the words, not just the denotations. Put it all together as you serve the following portion of the Word. It calls for lots of word color and generous use of the six P's as you orally interpret Holy Scripture. I demonstrate this passage on the DVD.

Daniel 5:1–12

King Belshazzar made a great feast for a thousand of his lords and drank wine in front of the thousand. Belshazzar, when he tasted the wine, commanded that the vessels of gold and of silver that Nebuchadnezzar his father had taken out of the temple in Jerusalem be brought, that the king and his lords, his wives, and his concubines might drink from them. Then they brought in the golden vessels that had been taken out of the temple, the house of God in Jerusalem, and the king and his lords, his wives, and his concubines drank from them. They drank wine and praised the gods of gold and silver, bronze, iron, wood, and stone.

Immediately the fingers of a human hand appeared and wrote on the plaster of the wall of the king's palace, opposite the lampstand. And the king saw the hand as it wrote. Then the king's color changed, and his thoughts alarmed him; his limbs gave way, and his knees knocked together. The king called loudly to bring in the enchanters, the Chaldeans, and the astrologers. The king declared to the wise men of Babylon, "Whoever reads this writing, and shows me its interpretation, shall be clothed with purple and have a chain of gold around his neck and shall be the third ruler in the kingdom." Then all the king's wise men came in, but they could not read the writing or make known to the king the interpretation. Then King Belshazzar was greatly alarmed, and his color changed, and his lords were perplexed.

The queen, because of the words of the king and his lords, came into the banqueting hall, and the queen declared, "O king, live forever! Let not your thoughts alarm you or your color change. There is a man in your kingdom in whom is the spirit of the holy gods. In the days of your father, light and understanding and wisdom like the wisdom of the gods were found in him, and King Nebuchadnezzar, your father—your father the king— made him chief of the magicians, enchanters, Chaldeans, and astrologers, because an excellent spirit, knowledge, and understanding to interpret dreams, explain riddles, and solve problems were found in this Daniel, whom the king named Belteshazzar. Now let Daniel be called, and he will show the interpretation."

6

Adding Some Spice

(Creative Methods)

It's a sin to bore people with the Bible.
— Haddon Robinson

B<small>Y NOW YOU</small> are able to serve healthy meals "simply" by reading with an informed mind and engaged heart. You are using your voice and body to orally interpret God's Holy Word. You already have a nourishing ministry, but to make your meals more tasty try adding some spice. None of the following should replace the standard ingredients discussed in previous chapters, but used judiciously they can add some zing. I have used nearly all of these in my ministries.

The "spices" are arranged in roughly ascending order from the common to the remarkable. Few churches will shy away from the methods at the beginning of the list, but you will have to discern if the methods at the end are too spicy for your culture. Don't try to force these on your congregation if people prefer a plain diet.

READ PASSAGES OTHER THAN THE ONE FOR THE SERMON. Stated negatively, stop treating the Scripture reading as only a preliminary to the sermon. Let the Word stand on its own legs.

LET SCRIPTURE PERVADE THE ENTIRE SERVICE. Use Scripture for the call to worship, invocation, prayer, and benediction. Try praying the psalms during the pastoral prayer.

DO RESPONSIVE READING. This is standard fare for many churches, and it is a fine way to get the congregation involved. If it is new to your group, try it with the reader and congregation alternating. If responsive reading is standard procedure for your group, mix it up a bit by having groups within the congregation read portions. For example, men–women; balcony–main floor; choir–congregation; parents–children. Some of the psalms are designed to be read antiphonally with one part of the congregation responding to the other part.

ASK THE CONGREGATION TO STAND FOR THE READING. This simple tool, already used by many churches, sanctifies the reading; that is, it "sets it apart" from the other elements of the service, thus focusing attention and heightening expectation.

SELECT A READER WHO EMBODIES THE TEXT. For example, have an expectant mother read the Magnificant (Luke 1), or a person who has experienced loss read the story of Lazarus (John 11). For Mother's Day, try an "intergenerational reading" with daughters, mothers, and grandmothers.

IMPORT "LESSONS AND CAROLS" FROM GREAT BRITAIN. This Christmas tradition is a simple service that intersperses Scripture and singing. That's all! Just Scripture and music—but it is lovely and inspiring.

GIVE LISTENERS A RESPONSE. As the people of God responded with "Amen, amen!" when Ezra read (Neh. 8), so can we. Punctuate the reading with "Allelujah," "We will do this!" or "Help us, Lord." Or give them a physical response such as bowing down, lifting hands, or lifting faces to heaven.

CREATE A "THEMATIC READING." Rather than reading a single passage, create a composite script using multiple verses on the same topic. Some of the sample scripts at the end of the book use a thematic approach, as does the one below on the theme of union with Christ.

> God chose me in Christ before he cre-
>   ated the world.
> He set me apart to be adopted through
>   Jesus Christ.
> God freely bestowed his grace on me in his
>   beloved Son,
>   forgiving my sins and setting me free
>   through the blood of Christ.
> He made me alive together with Christ
>   when I was dead in my sin.
>   He raised me up together with Christ,
>   and he has caused me to sit down to-

gether with Christ at his right hand in
heaven.
Nothing in all creation can separate me
from the love of God that is in Christ
Jesus my Lord.
Christ loves us and has freed us from our
sins by his blood.
Christ has disarmed the powers and au-
thorities, triumphing over them by the
cross,
and thus, I am free from bondage.
Christ will destroy every enemy, including
death, and establish his kingdom on
earth forever.
God has made known to us the mystery of
his will,
to sum up and bring together all things
in Christ.

READ TWICE USING DIFFERENT TRANSLATIONS. After
reading the translation of the pew Bibles, state,
"And now let me read the passage again in a different version." This increases attention, comprehension, and retention.

**WHEN PREACHING THROUGH AN ENTIRE BOOK, READ
THE PREVIOUS WEEK'S PASSAGE(S) AS WELL AS THE CUR-
RENT WEEK'S PASSAGE.** I did this when preaching
through First Corinthians. The series lasted about
thirty weeks, so we divided the book into five or
six units. Each unit had an average of five preaching texts. Our reading schedule looked like this:

Week	Reading Text (the reader read all of this)	Sermon Text (the congregation stood as the reader read this)
1	(Unit one) 1:1–9	(Unit one) 1:1–9
2	1:1–17	1:10–17
3	1:1–31	1:18–31
4	1:1–2:5	2:1–5
5	1:1–2:16	2:6–16
6	(Unit two) 3:1–9	(Unit two) 3:1–9
7	Etc.	Etc.

CONCLUDE THE SERMON WITH THE PASSAGE THAT WAS PREACHED. In making this suggestion, I am assuming that the passage was read before the sermon and then expounded in the sermon. Reading it as a conclusion is a satisfying experience for the listeners because they are able to see how the pieces make up the whole and the two readings "bookend" the message.

PROVIDE A BRIEF INTRODUCTION. Explain the context of the passage, vocabulary, or other issues unclear to listeners. In addition to preparing the listeners' minds, the introduction should also prepare their emotions. A few words that personalize the text and set the mood help with the task of bridge building. Too often we launch into our reading without allowing listeners to "warm up" mentally and emotionally.

COMMENT BRIEFLY ON THE TEXT AS YOU READ IT. This is similar to the previous suggestion, but it inserts parenthetic comments into the reading itself. For many people the Bible is hard to understand. Inserting brief explanatory comments can aid comprehension. I have heard British preacher Dick Lucas add the following parenthetic comment (note: to fully appreciate this example, you have to *hear* this austere and learned preacher with his polished English accent):

> Lot lifted up his eyes and saw that the Jordan Valley was well watered everywhere like the garden of the Lord. So Lot chose for himself all the Jordan Valley [pause] *foolish man* [pause] and Lot journeyed eastward.

Keep insertions short and use pauses to let the audience know that you are inserting your own words, or they may become confused.

JOIN PRIVATE READING AND PUBLIC TEACHING. Have people read the portion(s) of Scripture that will be taught in an upcoming sermon or class. My church did this when we preached through First Thessalonians. We encouraged people to read the entire book at least once a week for the duration of the nine-week series. I created bookmarks to keep track of the number of times they read First Thessalonians.

PRESENT THE PASSAGE FROM MEMORY. This simple technique can heighten the listeners' attention, but if it is foreign to your culture, it may seem like a performance calling attention to itself.

LEVERAGE THE POWER OF PROXEMICS. As mentioned in a previous chapter, this term means "the use of space for communication." For example, stand in the midst of the congregation when reading, have the people kneel while listening, sit while reading, place readers around the perimeter of the sanctuary, or use different levels or platforms. Unleash your creativity. As always, do not do these things merely because they are unusual, but because they enhance the reception of the Word.

RECITE AND MEMORIZE A VERSE EACH WEEK. When preaching a series, choose one verse per week that summarizes the theme of the sermon. Use various memorization techniques with the congregation, such as repeating the verse together, displaying part of it and having the people recite the rest, and reviewing regularly. My church did this when I preached a topical series called "Taming the Tongue."

Topic	Memory/theme verse
Intro: "The Power of the Tongue	Proverbs 18:21, "Death and life are in the power of the tongue, and those who love it will eat its fruit."
Complaining	Phil. 2:14, "Do everything without complaining."
Praise	Ps. 150:6, "Let everything that has breath praise the Lord. Praise the Lord!"

Topic	Memory/theme verse
Lying	Eph. 4:25, "Therefore, each of you must put off falsehood and speak truthfully with his neighbor, for we are all members of one body."
Speaking the Truth in Love	Same
Adult Language	Eph. 4:29, "Do not let any unwholesome talk come out of your mouths, but only what is helpful for building each other up."
Gossip	Prov. 18:8, "The words of a gossip are like choice morsels; they go down into the innermost parts of the body."
Encouragement	1 Thess. 5:11, "Therefore, encourage one another, and build each other up."
Flattery	Prov. 26:28, "A flattering mouth works ruin."
Words That Cut	Prov. 12:18, "Reckless words pierce like a sword, but the tongue of the wise brings healing."
Silence	Prov. 10:19, "When words are many, transgression is not lacking, but whoever restrains his lips is prudent."

HOLD A "BIBLE MARATHON." Professor Gary Friesen from Multnomah University does this regularly with students. They read aloud, in marathon sessions, portions of the Bible such as the entire New Testament or the Pentateuch.

INCORPORATE UNSCRIPTED RECITATION. Encourage people to speak verses of Scripture spontaneously. I have participated in meetings where this was done on topics such as the attributes of God, the power of the gospel, and prayer. The book of Ephesians indicates that "unscripted recitation" may have been done in the early church with singing, and it probably also was done with the quoting of Scripture: "Addressing one another in psalms and hymns and spiritual songs" (Eph. 5:19).

PROJECT THE TEXT ON SCREEN. This method of communication is a popular trend in North American churches. It has the advantage of letting people read with their eyes while hearing with their ears, and the use of two channels of communication is often beneficial. However, I have mixed feelings about the trend. We need pastoral and theological discernment on this issue. My home church has decided to not project the text (although we use the screen for other purposes) because we want congregants to bring their Bibles to church or at least use the pew Bibles. However, another trend is occurring: fewer and fewer folk are bringing their Bibles. Perhaps the two trends feed each other. If you choose to project the reading, make sure the font is large with plenty of margin around it. Also, the text should not appear before you start reading or attention will be split.

USE MUSIC. Have a guitarist or pianist play background music while you read. I did this when reading Psalm 77, pausing for the guitarist to play the "selah's" (which probably were musical interludes). Together we conveyed the mood of the poem. The background music could be pre-recorded, but live music is preferable. Another way to use music is to mix congregational singing, choir, or solo with the Scripture reading. For example, follow the reading with a hymn based on the text.

USE VISUAL ARTS. I know of a pastor in Oregon who preached through Ephesians, but on the final week of the series did not deliver a sermon. Instead, a skillful reader who had memorized the whole book presented it while a guitarist played and an artist, sketching on large panels, captured the ideas of the book. The congregation responded afterward with comments like this: "That was the most powerful presentation of Scripture I can remember."

If your church uses screens, you could project artwork. Imagine an Easter reading of the passion and resurrection of our Lord accompanied by classic works of art. Imagine a reading of the Prodigal Son (Luke 15) with Rembrandt's "Return of the Prodigal" displayed. With digital technology, you could even zoom in on portions of the painting— the Father's hands on the Prodigal's shoulder, or the Elder Son lurking in the background.

EXPERIMENT WITH LIGHTING. If the text warrants it and your church culture permits it, heighten the visual impact of your reading with light. For a Good Friday service, darken the sanctuary. For an Easter service, turn on the flood lights and add some color. For a striking use of torchlight, watch Charlton Heston reading from Genesis.[1] Inciden-

---

1. "Charlton Heston Presents the Bible," Good Times Home Video, 1993.

tally, most church platforms are poorly lit. This limits our ability to communicate with the tools of chapter 4, especially facial expression and eye contact.

TRY SOUND EFFECTS. The choir could murmur as Jesus instructs the Pharisees. A shofar could be sounded as Moses calls the people to assemble. Depending on how much freedom you have, you could even use taped effects such as night sounds underneath Nehemiah 2, a narrative that took place at night as Nehemiah inspected the walls of Jerusalem.

MIME THE TEXT OR USE SIGN LANGUAGE. You have probably seen this done with musical selections. Try it with public reading also. It uses the eye gate as well as the ear gate for passage of the Word.

These creative methods can add some spice to your ministry of the Word. The final chapter continues to add flavor by going into more detail on group reading.

7

Adding Some Spice

(Group Reading)

It was the duty of the trumpeters and singers to make themselves heard in unison with praise and thanksgiving to the Lord.

—2 Chronicles 5:13

IF YOU HAVEN'T experienced a group reading, think of it as roughly equivalent to the ministry of singing that can be done as solos, duets, ensembles, choirs, and so forth. The use of multiple voices creates more possibilities than does a single voice. A broader range of volume, options with proxemics and staging, and the heightened energy of group dynamics are some of the flavors that this spice adds.

The book of Second Chronicles captures some of those flavors. Imagine the host of Israel gathered at the dedication of the Temple as the Ark of the Covenant arrives. The singers are arrayed in fine linen. Banners wave, shofars sound, and incense rises as the Levites chant and the people shout. Solomon presides on a bronze platform, facing the altar and the people, standing at times and kneeling at times, spreading his hands to pray and to bless. The multisensory spectacle created awe and joy as the people worshiped the living God (see 2 Chronicles 5:13).

The previous chapter offered a spice rack of ideas for creative communication. This chapter follows with special focus on group reading.[1]

The suggestions are arranged in rough chronological sequence, beginning with the creation of the script and ending with an exhortation to practice. You will see some of the same advice found in previous chapters on solo reading. I mention it again here because of the special constraints of group reading.

CREATE THE SCRIPT TO BRING OUT THE IDEAS AND EMOTIONS OF THE TEXT. For example, after you have identified the climax of the passage, you could voice that section by having the entire group say the line in unison with full voice. If your study of the passage reveals a contrast of ideas, you could split the readers in two, giving a line to each side.

---

1. Remember to use the DVD to see the principles and techniques described. A group of readers demonstrate two of the sample scripts found at the end of this book.

If the text is full of pathos, begin with the whole group in unison, but then drop voices one at a time, slowing the rate until the final reader almost whispers. The possibilities are endless as you use the full range of the human voice. Remember to use proxemics as well. For example, to show a contrast, divide the group physically and have them move to two portions of the stage.

Creating the script demands that you use the skills of chapter 2. To convey ideas and emotions, we must understand those ideas, feel those emotions, and give life to that exegesis in the script. "Hear" the text in your mind and then translate that experience into your script. In addition to using standard tools like unison and solo voices, the speaking choir could also provide sound effects. They could hum "Lo, How a Rose Ere Blooming" underneath a reading from Isaiah, or provide an undercurrent of grumbling like the crowd as Jesus stands before Pilate.

INSERT "COMMENTARY" INTO THE SCRIPT. Adding your own words can flesh out the meaning of the text. For example, when the group is reading a psalm of thanksgiving, follow each verse by having the readers insert something they are thankful for. "I love you, O Lord, my strength" (Ps. 18:1) could be followed with "I love you, Lord because you gave me strength to trust you when I was in the hospital." "The Lord is my rock and my fortress" (Ps. 18:2) could be said in unison and then followed with a single voice stating, "You will be my fortress when I go to grad school this fall."

Blend the ancient and the modern. This is similar to the technique above and is demonstrated below with the script from Hebrews 11. The script begins with the heroes of faith in Hebrews 11 and then extends that line through church history to show that the long line of stalwart saints continues to this day. I once heard a group of teenagers read Proverbs 6 and 7 on sexual purity, inserting titles from magazine articles. Something like this:

Reader 1 (boy): My son, keep your father's commandment, and forsake not your mother's teaching.

Reader 2 (boy): "Best advice for kinky sex. Find out in this month's issue of *People* magazine."

Reader 3 (girl): At the window of my house I have looked out through the lattice and I have seen among the simple . . . a young man lacking sense . . . taking the road to her house."

Reader 4 (girl): "Twenty hot techniques to help you own him."

The juxtaposition of God's wisdom with the world's wisdom was jarring.

Don't use technique for the sake of technique. Having advocated creativity, now let me express the caution: Use technique only as a servant of the Word. Just because you have the ability to use multiple readers does not mean that you "have to" do so. Random voicing does not build a bridge from the text to the listeners.

PRINT THE SCRIPT SO THAT IT IS EASY TO READ. Use large, clear, and consistent fonts. Use spacing that makes the act of reading easy. Readers will have plenty to think about without having to decipher a crowded, jumbled, or confusing layout. Also, allow room in the margins for readers to make notes during rehearsals.

PLACE THE SCRIPTS IN PROFESSIONAL LOOKING FOLDERS. The standard practice in "readers theater" is to use medium-sized black folders. That works for our purposes too. Alternately, an Easter basket of colors could convey the mood of the resurrection. Or perhaps the scripts could be placed in Bibles. In any case, avoid using only sheets of paper. They are difficult to hold as they rustle and flop, and they look unprofessional. Never staple pages. They should be held in a three ring binder or something else that is secure and makes the turning of pages easy.

CHOOSE READERS WITH CARE. After you have created the script, you will know how many readers you need. Choose them carefully. Not everyone has the ability to embody ideas and emotions when they read in public. Just as you want people with musical ability to sing in your choir, you want people with speaking ability to read in your "speaking choir." Start with the reading group you have created (see chapter 3). Depending on the script, the group may be as small as two readers or as large as a large choir.

"BLOCK" THE READING TO CONVEY THOUGHTS AND EMOTIONS. The term "blocking" means using movement and positions on stage. Movement is likely to be minimal, but used judiciously it can help visually interpret the text. Some common movements are dividing the readers into two groups; having readers turn their backs to the audience, or turn profile; walking forward toward the congregation; using different levels such as the stairs in front of the platform; and positioning readers around the perimeter of the auditorium.

PRACTICE. If solo reading calls for practice (and it does), group reading calls for more. How much practice is necessary? The time-tested standard from theater should be our guide: one hour of rehearsal for every minute on stage.

My prayer is that the instruction of this book and DVD will increase the quantity and quality of Scripture reading in our churches. The Lord has given us the materials for a great feast, and we have the privilege of serving it with skill and humility.

Devote yourself to the public reading.

Sample Scripts

THE SCRIPTS ON the following pages include my commentary in a different font to show why I voiced and blocked them as I did. I have printed the first script twice—with commentary and without—so that you can see the actual script the readers used.

Psalm 148[1]
A Scripture Reading for Four Readers

Psalm 148 is an energetic and soaring poem of praise. To capture that energy and to bring out the poetry of Hebrew parallelism, I use a handful of techniques such as lines said in unison, one reader completing the thought which the previous one has started, and the addition of one voice at a time until all four readers trumpet the completed thought. With such short lines, you can see why rehearsal is crucial. All four voices, like the voices in a quartet, must communicate the same concept. All four readers must think the same thought even when they are silent so that when they join in there will be no choppy breaks in rhythm. This reading must be done with high energy and exquisite timing.

Reader(s)	Script with Commentary
All	Praise the Lord!
	Because this is the "headline" or "thesis" of the psalm, I have all four readers state it in unison with full voice.
1	Praise the Lord from the heavens,
	To capture the poetry of the Hebrew parallelism, I have given each reader half a line. One person states an idea, then the next person echoes that idea. The lines should be delivered by slightly overlapping the final words of the previous line, giving the performance momentum and energy.

---

1. The sample script uses NIV, whereas the rest of the book uses ESV.

Reader(s)	Script with Commentary
2	praise him from the skies.
	Notice how I arranged this script on the page. (This may be easier to see on the next script which is printed without commentary). I have indented lines which continue, thus helping the readers see that they are finishing a thought started by the preceding reader. Notice on the unmarked script below that I have the readers turn the page during a natural break rather than in the middle of a line that carries over from one reader to the next.
3	Praise him, all his angels,
4	Praise him, all the hosts of heaven.
All	Praise him,
2	sun and moon,
	Each repetition of "praise him" reverberates as all four readers trumpet the phrase.
All	Praise him,
3	twinkling stars.
	The script now jumps to verse seven. Because this reading was part of a choir performance and led into a song on God's power in creation, I edited Psalm 148 to bring out that aspect of His power and glory.
All	Praise the Lord
4	from the earth
1	your great sea creatures
2	and all ocean depths
Men	Lightning and hail,

Reader(s)	Script with Commentary
Women	Snow and storm
All	Wind and weather that obey him;
3	Mountains
add 1	and all hills
add 4	fruit trees
add 2	and all cedars
	Here the script uses the technique of adding one voice at a time, reaching mini-climaxes until the final crescendo of verse 14 in the unison lines below.
3	Wild animals,
add 1	and all livestock,
add 4	reptiles,
add 2	and birds;
All	Kings of the earth and all people, rulers and judges of the earth; let them all praise the name of the Lord! For his name is very great. His glory towers over the earth and heaven.

Psalm 148
A Scripture Reading for Four Readers

Reader(s)	Script
All	Praise the Lord!
1	Praise the Lord from the heavens,
2	praise him from the skies.
3	Praise him, all his angels,
4	Praise him, all the hosts of heaven.
All	Praise him,
2	sun and moon,
All	Praise him,
3	twinkling stars.
All	Praise the Lord
4	from the earth
1	your great sea creatures
2	and all ocean depths
Men	Lightning and hail,
Women	Snow and storm
All	Wind and weather that obey him;
3	Mountains
add 1	and all hills
add 4	fruit trees
add 2	and all cedars

Reader(s)	Script
3	Wild animals,
add 1	and all livestock,
add 4	reptiles,
add 2	and birds;
All	Kings of the earth and all people, rulers and judges of the earth; let them all praise the name of the Lord! For his name is very great. His glory towers over the earth and heaven.

Revelation 7:9–12
A Scripture Reading for
Choir and Four Readers

This script is similar to the previous one. In this one, the four readers performed while standing in front of the choir. I gave the entire choir some emphatic lines, and the effect was awe-inspiring.

The readers and choir members memorized this script.

Reader(s)	Script
1	I looked before me and there was a great multitude that no one could count, from every nation
2	tribe,
3	people,
4	and language,
1	standing before the throne
3	and in front of the Lamb.
2	They were wearing white robes
4	and were holding palm branches in their hands
	Gestures could be used here and other places to convey the ideas.
1–4	And they cried out with a loud voice:
Choir & Readers	Salvation belongs to our God, who sits upon the throne, and to the Lamb.
	The choir and readers must be coached to "let it all out" on this line. They must proclaim it with conviction. The phrasing can be done a few different ways and you should experiment in rehearsals with which one sounds best. We put a slight pause after "who sits upon the throne."

Reader(s)	Script
2	All the angels were standing around the throne
4	and around the elders
1	and the four living creatures
3	They fell down on their faces before the throne and worshipped God, saying:
	The following lines use the technique we saw in the previous script—adding voices. In this case, the script first adds a single reader, then it adds all the readers, then part of the choir (tenors and altos) and then the full choir. When well rehearsed, the effect is powerful.
1	Amen!
add 4	Praise and glory
add other readers	and wisdom and thanks and honor
add tenors and altos	and power and strength
all	be to our God for ever and ever. Amen!
	The piano immediately began the intro to the choir's next song; thus the Scripture reading and the music formed a seamless spiritual and aesthetic experience.

Ransomed: A Reading for Five Readers

This script was also memorized. This script is topical, dealing with the doctrine of Christ's substitutionary death. It is explanatory as well as doxological, thus it teaches even as it inspires. The verses in parenthesis are not stated. They are in the script just to show the readers where the words come from since I also include my own words along with the words of the Bible.

In contrast to the previous scripts, this one is more contemplative. It should be performed with a slower rate.

You will see indications of simple blocking as well as mime. Thus this performance includes rudimentary elements of drama.

Reader(s)	Script
All	He gave himself as a ransom for all. (1 Tim. 2:6)
1, 3, 5	He gave himself as a ransom for all.
2	He gave *himself* . . .
3	as a *ransom* . . .
4	for us.
All	What is a "ransom"?
1	A ransom is a payment,
5	something valuable,
3	something of worth.
1	A ransom is a substitute,
2	An exchange,
4	a price paid to release a hostage.
1	Why do we need a ransom?

Reader(s)	Script
5	Because without Christ, we are slaves:
	The next speeches are directed to the audience; during them the four readers who are not speaking strike attitudes which illustrate the Scripture being quoted. For example, during the lines dealing with redemption, the four readers gather to one side. With wrists crossed, they suggest slavery; then at an appropriate point, they are "released."
5	He redeemed us, not with corruptible things like silver or gold . . . but with the precious blood of Christ. (1 Peter 1:18)
	Readers quickly reassemble in a different position: hands cover faces and shoulders hunch in weakness. As reader 5 reads the second half of the speech, they stand erect and look up to God.
5	A ransom was paid because we are sick: You see, at just the right time, when we were still powerless, Christ died for the ungodly. (Romans 5:6)
	Readers form a line, shoulder to shoulder, and turn their backs to the audience. On "gains access" reader 5 walks through them as through a door, and they turn to face audience.

Reader(s)	Script
5	We need a ransom because we are enemies of God, shut out from his presence. But we have been justified through faith; we have peace [readers turn] with God through our Lord Jesus Christ, through whom we have gained access [5 walks through]. (Romans 5:1)
	During the first half of the following speech, reader 4 stands tall and points disapprovingly at 3, who cowers in guilt. Then, as 5 finishes the speech, another reader goes to 4, gently pulls down his or her arm, raises 3, and joins their hands.
5	The ransom was necessary because we stand guilty before a Holy God. But if anyone sins, we have an advocate with the Father, Jesus Christ the righteous. (1 John 2:1)
	All readers face the audience. The final lines are delivered progressively slowly so that the climax comes not with a crash but with a gentle settling.
1	He gave himself as a ransom for all (1 Tim. 2:6).
1, 3, 5	He gave *himself. . .*
4	as a *ransom . . .*
1	for you
2	and me.

Hebrews 11
An Adaptation for Four Readers

This script calls for little blocking but great energy and flexibility of voice. As with most group readings, the lines should be delivered so that they slightly overlap. The group must communicate with one mind and heart. The reading begins slowly and then picks up steam as it progresses. Toward the end, as the climax approaches, all four readers ham-mer the lines assigned to "All."

Reader(s)	Script
1	We are surrounded by witnesses,
4	surrounded by witnesses.
2	Daniel who prayed with his windows flung open.
3	Peter and John who said, "We must obey God rather than men."
1	Moses who refused to be known as the son of Pharaoh's daughter.
4	Abraham, who did not know where he was going.
1	But he obeyed and went,
4	for he was looking for the city which has foundations,
1	whose architect and builder is God. (Heb. 11:8-10)
2	Esther, who would not live in comfort while her people were murdered,
3	but said, "I will go to the king,
2	though it is against the law.
3	And if I perish,
2	I perish." (Esther 4:16).
1	We don't have time to tell about Gideon,

Reader(s)	Script
2	Barak,
4	Samson,
1	Jephthah,
3	David,
2	Samuel,
1	and the prophets;
4	John the Baptist,
2	John the Apostle,
3	Peter,
2	and Paul;
1	Augustine,
4	Martin Luther,
2	Hudson Taylor,
4	Jim Eliot,
3	the believers behind the Iron Curtain,
1	and the suffering saints today in Sudan.
2	Through faith they conquered kingdoms,
3	administered justice,
1	and gained what was promised;
	The energy increases. The lines start to tumble over each other.
4	They shut the mouths of lions,
2	quenched the fury of the flames,
1	and escaped the edge of the sword;
3	whose weakness was turned to strength,
1	who became powerful in battle
3	and routed foreign armies.
2	Women received back their dead,
3	raised to life again.

Reader(s)	Script
4	Others were tortured and refused to be released,
2	so that they might gain a better resurrection.
1	Some faced jeers and flogging;
3	others were chained and put in prison.
2	They were
All	stoned;
2	They were
All	sawed in two;
2	They were
All	put to death by the sword.
3	They went about in sheepskins and goatskins,
3, 4	destitute,
2, 3, 4	persecuted,
All	and mistreated.
3	The world was not worthy of them.
1	These were all commended for their faith.
3	They ran the race with patience.
4	We are surrounded by a great cloud of witness,
1	Therefore, let us
All	throw off
1	everything that hinders,
2	And the sin that so easily besets us.
4	And let us run with patience the race marked out for us.
3	Let us fix our eyes on Jesus,
4	the author and perfecter of our faith,

Reader(s)	Script
3	Who for the joy set before him
1	endured the cross,
2	scorning its shame,
3	and sat down at the right hand of the throne of God. *Pause and slow down. Bring the reading to a close.*
4	Consider him who endured such opposition from sinful men,
2	so that you will not grow weary and lose heart.

Be Creative in Your Preaching!

ISBN 978-0-8254-2019-1
Available from www.kregel.com or wherever books are sold